REGULATING INTERNATIONAL STUDENTS' WELLBEING

Gaby Ramia, Simon Marginson and Erlenawati Sawir

First published in Great Britain in 2013 by

Policy Press
University of Bristol
Fourth Floor
Beacon House
Queen's Road
Bristol BS8 1QU
UK
t: +44 (0)117 331 4054
f: +44 (0)117 331 4093
tpp-info@bristol.ac.uk
www.policypress.co.uk

North America office:
Policy Press
c/o The University of Chicago Press
1427 East 60th Street
Chicago, IL 60637, USA
t: +1 773 702 7700
f: +1 773-702-9756
sales@press.uchicago.edu
www.press.uchicago.edu

British Library Cataloguing in Publication Data
A catalogue record for this book is available from the British Library.

Library of Congress Cataloging-in-Publication Data
A catalog record for this book has been requested.

ISBN 978 1 44731 015 0 hardcover

FSC
www.fsc.org
MIX
From responsible sources
FSC® C018575

Contents

List of tables and figures

Tables

Figures

Acknowledgements

In undertaking the writing of this book we are indebted first and foremost to colleagues who have worked alongside us over a number of years. The book is part of a longer and larger collaborative story, and those colleagues have written with us on other projects, informing and enhancing our understanding of the questions with which we deal here. They have conversed with us over many an hour on wider and related issues and for that we thank them. By name and affiliation they are: Professor Chris Nyland of Monash University, who led a large team of researchers at that institution when we were all on staff there, on broader questions of global people mobility. Dr Helen Forbes-Mewett, also from Monash, was a valued colleague and collaborator in international education. Sharon Smith, now of the City of Melbourne, contributed vital research support and important discussions on how students live in host communities. Kathleen Mendan from Monash and Nicholas Bromfield from the University of Sydney provided excellent research assistance.

Gaby Ramia is the lead author and bears the main responsibility for the book. We have benefited tremendously from the support offered by our current institutional departments and universities. For Gaby, this is the Graduate School of Government, University of Sydney. For Simon Marginson, it is the Centre for the Study of Higher Education, University of Melbourne. For Erlenawati Sawir, it is the International Education Research Centre, Central Queensland University (Melbourne). No person or institution acknowledged here is responsible for any omissions or errors of argument or judgement.

Finally we would like to thank the staff of Policy Press, in particular Emily Watt, senior commissioning editor, and Laura Vickers, senior editorial assistant. We are very happy indeed to have our work associated with Policy Press. They guided us through a thoroughly rigorous and engaging but always respectful process of submission, reviewers, response, consideration, revision and finally, publication.

Preface

Among the primary benefits of international education for nations receiving students, the host country, is the contribution to exports. Education across borders also facilitates international cultural exchange, and is a contributor to positive diplomatic and economic relations. If students return to their home country after completing their studies, an international education represents vital investment in intellectual capital. The importance of this is, of course, greatest for developing countries, from where a disproportionately large proportion of students hail. So, in the context of a global knowledge economy, both education exporters and importers stand to benefit. One of the many ingredients of an emergent cosmopolitan world and peaceful society must arguably be the phenomenon of students travelling from one country to another to pursue education. Students can make excellent unpaid ambassadors for their home country and culture, not just while undertaking studies but also in professional positions post-graduation.

International education offers mixed blessings, however. Few host countries provide adequately for the welfare of incoming students, who contribute enormously to the cultural and economic fabric of their host societies. One of our primary motivations in writing this book is our perception, backed up by analysis, that international students are too often constructed by policy makers as market participants exercising free choice, and not as people who, while internationally mobile, are nevertheless economically and socially vulnerable. Their vulnerability impels us to explore the moral questions surrounding the responsibilities of nations that profit so much economically. We seek to show how student vulnerability plays out, what it looks like, and more importantly, how the regulatory protections afforded international students in a host country are not true to the welfare services and provisions promised in legislation and accompanying documentation. We do not ignore students' own responsibilities and agencies.

Our primary conceptual focus is regulation, both formal and informal, and our countries of central interest are Australia and New Zealand. These two nations benefit enormously from export revenues and indeed are among the world leaders on that score, but they do not deliver on the undertaking of the wellbeing of international students. Notwithstanding important and in the main well-founded news headlines alleging that international students have been victim to racism and exploitation in areas such as housing and employment, both Australian and New Zealand policy makers seem content to continue exporting services while not substantively attending to the human welfare deficits that too often beset markets. Having said that, we do not want to suggest that other countries are free from fundamental policy problems, and we do discuss several other nations in the earlier chapters to set the context for the Australia–New Zealand comparison that then takes centre-stage in the middle chapters, making way for global implications in the latter parts.

While we find that New Zealand's approach is superior to Australia's when assessed according to the letter of formal regulatory instruments, on the basis of extensive interviews in each country with students and support service providers and policy makers, we argue that analysts and practitioners in international education need to dig deeper to assess the impact of welfare. They must interrogate when, how, and in many cases, if, students access support. They should ask questions of the primary participants themselves about how the support structures operate and in the process assess whether governments are credibly, substantively committed to delivering student wellbeing.

Echoing the warnings of scholars in other areas, we argue that formal regulation is not what it seems. What appears to be mainly behind it is market opportunity maximisation rather than student rights. We need to think twice and to analyse not just the wording of government interventions, but also the effects on regulatory human subjects, who are, in our sphere, global market participants. We know in the contemporary climate all too well that markets are subject to crisis and downturn. We need not simply swallow the assumption that economic 'good times' in international education will always prevail. One of the best ways to manage risk in this domain is to pay attention to the student welfare dimension, which is worthy of analysis in its own right and independent of economic, trade, diplomatic, foreign policy and marketing concerns.

ONE

Introduction: global students and their discontents

China goes to New Zealand: a morality tale

Each year a growing number of college and university students are travelling to foreign countries (nations other than the nation in which they hold citizenship rights) in order to study. Between 2000 and 2010 the worldwide number of foreign students increased from 2.1 million to 4.1 million, an expansion of 99 per cent in only a decade (OECD, 2011, p 364). Total student mobility is much greater, as it also includes students who travel for semester-length programmes or on short-term student exchanges. In short, international education is part of the biography of more and more people. It has become a key phase in life, the passport to a new environment and career, and even perhaps a new identity.

While the growth of international education has been rapid, the expansion has not been the same everywhere. Like most social trends it is subject to fits and starts and appears 'lumpy', accumulating in some places rather than others. Certain nations produce large numbers of students on the move, and certain nations specialise in educating them, while other nations remain relatively untouched. As we discuss in Chapter Four, in the early 2000s, among the world's fastest growing providers of international education were the Asia-Pacific nations Australia and New Zealand. Although New Zealand started a bit later than Australia, growth became even more rapid, largely fuelled by China, with New Zealand being marketed vigorously, for a time, by education agents in China. A growing number of Chinese families had the means to pay for foreign education, and an English language education offered definite advantages, especially to families working in the export businesses driving much of China's growth. New Zealand was seen as safe and clean, cheaper than the other English language countries, with a reputation for multicultural tolerance and strong educational institutions with roots in British schooling and universities.

At first the rapid growth in the number of Chinese students was trouble free. Chinese families were eager to take up the opportunity and the dollars flowed in. The export industry seemed to be a 'win-win' for everyone. But not everyone in New Zealand was comfortable with the influx of new faces, and a disquieting pattern of stereotyping and hostile media coverage developed (Collins, 2006). Increasingly 'Chinese students', or 'Asian students' (a widely used synonym for 'Chinese students') found themselves front page or page 3 news in the tabloids. The use of the generic categories swept up and 'Othered' every student in New Zealand who came from East Asia, Southeast Asia, South Asia or the Middle East. Reports highlighted the involvement of 'Asian students' in alleged crimes. Chinese students were said to be bad drivers, a new threat to safety on the New Zealand roads. They had poor communication skills. They were lowering the standard of tertiary education. They were crowding into unsanitary inner-city dwellings. 'Asian street smells' from non-European restaurants in the largest city, Auckland, were destroying the traditional urban ambience. In other words, 'Asian students' were incompatible with the New Zealand way of life. This was undefined, but seemed to be something understood by many. Reports about the involvement of Chinese students in crime, whether as perpetrators or victims, proved to be especially potent and were frequently repeated. It seemed that even when Chinese students were victims of crime, this was, in some sense, their fault, and served to highlight their un-New Zealand character, their 'Otherness', their essential nature as unwelcome outsiders.

No doubt it all helped to sell newspapers. But the lurid media creation of a Chinese outsider at the heart of New Zealand society, supported by a continuing flow of reports of alarming incidents, generated ongoing insecurity among both visitors and citizens. This undermined New Zealand's claim to safety and quietude, which had been its marketing edge over the US and the UK. It also triggered alarm bells in China itself. The Chinese government consistently maintains an interest in the welfare of people from China abroad, and in 2003 Chinese Embassy officials advised the New Zealand government that they were dissatisfied with the level of attention being given to the safety of Chinese students (Li, 2007). China was concerned about the paucity of provision for student safety, the creation of fraudulent education suppliers and hostile media coverage and the racial vilification of Asians.

The response of the New Zealand government in Wellington was to claim that all was well in the best of all possible worlds. The government pointed to New Zealand's existing regulatory framework, as if that was sufficient argument in itself. New Zealand nominally provided for the pastoral care of international students through the regulation of provider education institutions. Universities and colleges were bound by the government's *Code of practice for the pastoral care of international students* (MOENZ, 2011a), and if students were unhappy with the treatment they received, they could complain to the International Education Appeal Authority (IEAA). However, proclaiming business as usual by pointing to the virtues of existing regulation neglected two inconvenient facts. First, business as usual was not working. Second, the regulation of providers could offer no purchase on students' sense of wellbeing in the general community beyond the reach of the educational institutions. Nor did the government seek to counter the stereotypes circulating in the newspapers, although these were dominating the debate. Instead it stepped up its marketing around the theme that New Zealand was a safe venue for international education.

This was a serious miscalculation. With New Zealand regulators in avoidance mode, and thus with no other means of influencing the position of Chinese students in New Zealand, China's Ministry of Education pulled the rug, branding New Zealand as unable to protect Chinese students, and posting this advisory on its website:

> In recent years, the number of Chinese full fee-paying students studying in New Zealand is increasing rapidly. The number reached over 30,000 by the end of 2002. New Zealand's limited number of tertiary institutions, its inadequate transport and infrastructure do not have capacity to accommodate such a large number of international students. Most Chinese students are very young and study low-level subjects and courses. They do not have a sense of self-control and self-protection. Therefore, there are many problems with these Chinese students, such as tension with homestay families, traffic offences, violence, prostitution, gambling, crimes, fraudulence, drugs, kidnapping, and murdering. (Chinese Ministry of Education, cited by Li, 2007)

The number of students from China entering New Zealand went into free-fall. Total international students from all source countries combined dropped from 126,919 in 2002 to 92,246 in 2005 (ENZ, 2011). The decline triggered a spate of research on the nature of the risks affecting international students, and how to restore New Zealand's reputation as a provider of safe conditions (Butcher and McGrath, 2004; Ward and Masgoret, 2004; Jackson, 2005; Lewis, 2005; Collins, 2006;

Xi and Ning, 2006; Tan and Simpson, 2008). The government moved to strengthen *The code of practice*, imposing on education institutions a stronger strategy for reputation management. It even discussed measures to enhance actual student safety (McGrath et al, 2008). But it was to be some years before total international enrolments climbed back, and while numbers from nations other than China increased sharply, numbers from China have not fully recovered.

This debacle over Chinese students in New Zealand was instructive. The New Zealand government's first response was telling, falling back on the habits of marketing strategies and the devolution of problems to education providers rather than taking an open political approach; and it evaded responsibility for the moral dimension of the problem. This says much about the philosophy of state underpinning the governance and regulation of international education in New Zealand. The New Zealand stance was typical of a neoliberal state soaked in traditions of limited government and fascinated by its own commercialisation strategy. Yet the response also said something about the lacuna in the regulation of all international education, in all countries, regardless of philosophy or political traditions. The boundary between citizen and non-citizen is crucial to this industry, the product of which is often the first step to permanent migration. And that boundary enables the commercial providers of international education to ignore the broader human rights of students and to treat them mainly as consumers. That boundary also produces a fractured regulatory framework, dysfunctional not only in relation to rights but also in terms of a sustainable and stable market.

It was easy for New Zealand to sidestep the political and moral issues by drawing the national boundary and treating international education, whose students fell outside the bounds of national citizenship, mainly as a commercial problem. Even this thoroughly neoliberal regime could not have positioned its own citizen students *solely* as consumers without a broader identity and set of rights, nor could it have let media and public stereotyping of its own citizens go unchallenged. The government in Wellington was never going to be criticised by its own media for neglecting 'Asian students', but it would have run a political risk if seen to undermine the imagined white utopia of the 'Anglo-New Zealand'. The 'security' of an imaginary New Zealand tradition weighed larger than the security of non-citizen foreign students, despite the revenues provided by the foreigners. And so the beleaguered students from China were left with nowhere to go but home. China and Chinese families responded to the failure of regulation, and the market collapsed.

This incident suggests other lessons for the governance and regulation of international education. First, the 'Asian student' was largely silent throughout. It is difficult for non-citizen international students to exercise political agency (more so when they lack full communicative competence), especially without an explicit guarantee of comprehensive rights. This underlines the point that consumer rights that with difficulty enable the student to call the educational provider to account are not a viable platform from which to challenge media stereotyping. Second, the welfare factors left outside of, or incompletely covered by, the framework of commercial regulation, with its notion of the student as consumer, can be very substantial in human terms. In this case a range of matters are given scant, if any, attention, from international student safety from crime, to relations with the New Zealand community on the roads, and the negative effects of hostile and reductionist media treatment. Third, not only is the commercial bias of international education regulation unable to fully comprehend the political and social dimensions of international students' lives, but all systems governance and regulation find it difficult to reach fully into the informal, private sectors, without adopting unacceptable forms of surveillance and intervention. Finally, the students' own national government can enter the fray on their behalf, for government cannot use its own regulatory instruments on another government's soil. It is left with diplomatic prodding, which may not work and cannot outweigh national political and economic concerns, or blunt political or commercial sanctions such as the website advisory cited above. Only the government in the country of education is in a position to manage comprehensively the welfare of international students.

Global student market

Does it matter what happens to Chinese students in the small and geographically isolated nation of New Zealand? Apart from the obvious point that it matters if you are in New Zealand, or if you are from China and thinking about going to New Zealand, it matters because of the global issues invoked. International education in New Zealand and its neighbour Australia have a special importance at this time. In the last two decades they have been at the cutting edge of global student mobility, and are playing a key role in the rapidly growing, world-scale market.

The 4.5 million people of New Zealand inhabit two large and eight much smaller islands located in the southwest Pacific Ocean, five hours to the east of the time zones of Shanghai and Singapore.

Its nearest continental neighbour, located on the western edge of the Pacific and just south of Indonesia in Asia, is Australia, where 22.8 million people occupy a larger landmass, almost the size of the US. Australia is more arid than the US, with most of the population on the east and southern coasts. Both New Zealand and Australia were British colonial foundations. They inherited English as their primary language and have developed the robust tertiary education systems common to the English-speaking world. Australia has 19 universities ranked in the world top 500 research universities and New Zealand has five such institutions.

Although these countries are far from the older Atlantic power centres, in a world now shaped by greater global connectedness, together with the spectacular rise of Asia, they have, for the first time, assumed a larger world role in education. In 2010 Australia (6.6 per cent of the world market) and New Zealand (1.7 per cent) between them educated one in twelve of the world's cross-border tertiary students. Issues that have emerged in international education in Australia and New Zealand have implications – and perhaps lessons – for the longer established international education nations of the US (16.6 per cent), the UK (13 per cent), Germany (6.6 per cent), France (6.3 per cent), Canada (4.7 per cent), Russia (3.9 per cent) and other European nations. As noted, these issues also have resonances in Asia, where China, Japan, Malaysia and Singapore both send and receive international students. Japan housed 3.4 per cent of the world's foreign students in 2010 and 1.8 per cent were studying in China (OECD, 2011, p 364).

At the same time, these issues are new and not yet well understood. As we discuss in this book, policy and regulatory systems are poorly equipped for handling this cross-border movement of students on a mass scale, just as they are poorly equipped to handle the mass movement of some other globally mobile people such as refugees and temporary workers. But where has mass international education come from? Why are an increasing number of students crossing borders in this way? What are the challenges created by their mobility for the nation of education and for the students themselves?

With their relatively small national markets, Australia and New Zealand have been highly dependent on trade since 19th-century colonial times. In the last 20 years, a major newcomer in the services sector, international education, has joined their traditional exports in technologically intensive agriculture, minerals and energy. In these two countries together, more than one student in five is a foreigner who crossed into the country in order to obtain an education and has been granted a temporary student visa. Most of these foreign students are from Asia, with China the largest single source country, and large numbers of students also from India, Malaysia, Singapore, Vietnam and Indonesia. Nearly all of these students pay full-cost tuition fees and generate revenues for the colleges and universities that educate them. International education has become a business in Australia and New Zealand, as in the UK, China, Malaysia, Singapore, and in much of Europe and North America.

International education is not only global; it is also rapidly growing. This is a sign of the global times in which business reaches across national borders, professional labour is more mobile, people travel much more often for work, business investment, tourism and family reasons, and communications and cultures everywhere are tending to converge, although important cultural and linguistic differences remain and help to give form and content to the globality. Meanwhile, emerging Asian nations have become the chief drivers of worldwide economic growth, and the middle classes in the two most populous nations, China and India, are expanding each decade by numbers equivalent to a large European nation. A proportion of these emerging middle-class families want English language skills and education, and to acquire these more fully by student immersion in an English-speaking country, as well as the formative experience of learning to survive in another country. Internationally mobile students remain only a small proportion of the Asian population, yet given the demographic weight of China and India, even 1 per cent of the domestic student population becomes a large number of mobile students in other nations.

International student wellbeing and regulation

In their host countries international students have become part of the educational fabric, and part of the social, cultural and economic landscape in the inner cities and suburbs. Many study, live, eat, make friends, engage in recreation, use public transport and often also work part time for some years. Those whose incomes reach a threshold level pay taxes to their host country government, although they do not enjoy the status of citizens. And they are doing all of this in increasing numbers. In the late 1980s in Australia, in all sectors of education and training, there were about 20,000 international students. One generation later the number exceeds 600,000 a year. In Australia and New Zealand taken together, the international student population constitutes about 3 per cent of all residents but a much higher proportion of the population of the inner urban population, especially among those living near university sites. Like all migrants, temporary or permanent, international students tend to 'clump' in certain suburbs close to each other. The same happens in the UK and Canada.

However, despite their numerical prominence, the lives, needs, issues, challenges and problems of this large group of temporary migrants have been little researched. Most studies of international students focus on the factors affecting academic success and/or the 'adjustment' of international students to the norms of the host country, or their 'satisfaction' as consumers in a global market (see, for example, Barrie, 2006; Montgomery and McDowell, 2008; Monash University, 2008; Universities Australia, 2008; see the fuller literature review in Marginson et al, 2010). Little attention is given to international students in their own right, to their needs as opposed to satisfaction levels, or to the 'adjustment' of host nations to them. This lack of balance in the literature reflects the fact that international students are seen essentially as outsiders in their host environment. They are rarely seen as human agents in the full sense, as deserving of equal rights and respect, albeit on a temporary basis for the duration of their stay (Marginson, 2011b). There is no need to adjust to the foreign student, it seems, because she/he is here in the country by grace and favour, he/she is temporary, and as we discuss in this book (it seems that this is the bottom line in matters of respect and rights) she/he is not 'one of us'. Although international students are a large population in countries such as Australia, New Zealand and the UK, in a curious sense they are also largely invisible.

Host countries use a number of sometimes contrary, confused and myth-laden lenses to view international students. None of these delivers a full, or fully empathetic, picture. International students are temporary migrants and student visa holders, yes, but a threat to national security because temporary visa holders are liable to overstay. International students work too hard and are unnaturally ambitious and competitive; or they are students whose command of English is imperfect and whose very presence threatens to drive down standards; or, if their teaching is more adequate, they foster the neglect of local students seen as 'more deserving' of the attention of educators. They are part-time workers whose desperate material circumstances and low expectations make them willing to be exploited, with notoriously low wages and poor conditions, threatening to undermine local workers. They are wealthy – surely they must be, to afford those tuition fees? – and less than fully responsible young people whose parents squander on them new cars and expensive flats. They are members of families whose dependents are overloading the health system. Yet whole dimensions of their lives are missing.

Security and agency

What is the state of international students' wellbeing? While in the country of education, to what extent and in which domains can international students exercise effective rights?

The first study to examine international student welfare and agency on a comprehensive basis was published as *International student security* (Marginson et al, 2010). Arguably, the main conceptual contribution of that work was that it conceived of the international student as an active self-determining agent, rather than as a passive welfare subject dependent solely on external care. It did not ignore welfare needs; rather it saw them as agency-dependent, sustained by a combination of self-resources and external conditions, including those provided by government and community organisations, as well as by provider institutions. 'Human security' is defined in Marginson et al (2010) as the stable capacity to exercise human agency. This governs the approach to its empirical research.

The research team identified a number of interlocking domains of activity bearing on the human security of international students. As well as the academic learning setting, these domains included communications, finances, work, accommodation, safety of the person, health, relations with authorities in government and education, personal networks, engagement with local students, and engagement in the general community, including intercultural relations and problems of discrimination and abuse. The research was conducted in Australia alone in 2004-08, and consisted of a review of relevant research literature in each of these security domains, a study of contemporary documents and a large body of interviews with international students (200), together with interviews with local students.

International student security identified 28 ways in which the regulated position of international students was inferior to that of local students in Australia. These included access to public financial support and to some private banking services, the cost of public transport (international students were not eligible for student concession fares in parts of the country where the majority of students lived), the cost of public schooling for students' children, the cost of health cover, the right to work (international students were and are limited to 20 hours per week), and political rights, where the visas of some international students restricted political activity. Similar although not identical differentiation occurred in other countries that educated international students. Data from the interviews with international students suggested that the international student experience differed from the local student experience in some important ways.

First, the majority of internationals in Australia faced at least some difficulties and barriers in communicating in English. Communication is key to active agency and cross-cultural relations and to learning, and language-related difficulties are the most frequently reported item in research on international students in English-speaking countries. These problems affected not just the academic progress of some interviewees, but their daily lives and especially cross-cultural relations. Second, and related but not identical to the language issue, there were pronounced differences in areas where cultural identity was at play, not just in cross-cultural relations but in looking for rental housing, and other key public sphere activities such as looking for a job. Third, international students faced the challenges of dealing with the immigration department, which was notorious for poor interpersonal relations. Local students never have to deal with that department. Fourth, as this problem indicates, internationals were outsiders, non-citizens. On the whole their lives were more marginal, lonelier and less well recognised. Many were affected by pronounced loneliness, particularly early on in their stay, and a significant minority were relatively isolated throughout the student sojourn. This outsider status affected them profoundly in many areas of life.

In other respects the experiences of international students seemed to be broadly similar to those of local students. They faced a complex mix of similarity and difference. For example, a minority of international students faced serious financial difficulties, perhaps a third of all interviewees. This was similar to the proportion of local students found in other studies. So many international students had to work. Some internationals faced exploitation and abuse at work, in forms and with severities not faced by their local counterparts. The international student experience was also distinct because of the fact that their visas limited them to only 20 hours work a week during a semester. This not only limited their earning powers, it rendered them especially vulnerable to exploitation by employers. It was evident that some students worked more than 20 hours a week. If they complained about their working conditions they could be threatened with exposure to the immigration authorities. It was not always so explicit, but there was a tacit threat. Likewise, international students and local students both faced neglectful and exploitative landlords in the private rental market. But international students had a special vulnerability. In the market for rental accommodation in Sydney and Melbourne there was a severe shortage of supply. It was a seller's market and several interviewees had experienced discrimination within the market. A further problem was the extreme information asymmetries affecting newcomers. Often international students lacked information about the housing market when they signed up for high rent rooms in poor conditions early on in their stay.

Most of the international students who were interviewed said that forming friendships with local students had proven harder than expected. This was one of the strongest findings of the Marginson et al (2010) study. Locals tended to self-segregate. They saw no need to move out of their comfort zone. This also encouraged international students to self-segregate, reinforcing the initial survival strategies that many had adopted. The main outcome was separation between the two broad groups of students, but other pathologies also developed. In total, 99 of the 200 students interviewed in Australia – that is, just under 50 per cent – said they had experienced cultural hostility or prejudice while in Australia. The rate was especially high for students from Singapore and Malaysia and above average for students from China. The perception of hostility or prejudice was higher for women than for men. Although there were a small number of complaints about administrative or academic staff, by far the overwhelming majority of problems occurred outside the campus. A large proportion of interviewees had been abused on the street or on public transport. This could also happen in shops, and in students' workplaces, dealing with local customers, and sometimes when dealing with the boss. Several students reported unprovoked abusive incidents that had profoundly distressed them. In these incidents they were made to feel alien, often with lasting effect. Further, in such cases there was no process for claiming rights and for seeking redress. They needed more than comfort and support; they needed to reassert their dignity and agency, to claim the right to respect and to belonging, but they often could not. Some blamed this on the universities. Some blamed it on the government. Others blamed it on themselves, or blamed no one, and felt the psychological consequences of doing so.

As we make clear below, this current study makes reference to *International student security* but takes the Australian data it reported on as a given. Here we focus squarely on the ways in which international students in Australia and in New Zealand are affected by formal and informal regulation. To support this objective the current analysis uses data from interviews with national regulators, university personnel and outside service providers, drawing trans-national and global regulatory implications. This kind of analysis has thus far been absent in the international education literature, not only in relation to Australia and New Zealand, but in other places too.

Governance and regulation

An additional unique feature of this current work lies in the application of 'governance and regulation' to international education, which we define in wider terms than just national or local rule and norm-setting systems. As noted, the complex regulatory problem created by international education is that international students move between two national jurisdictions; in addition, the two are often culturally different. Students are citizens in one jurisdiction, the home country, but their daily lives are largely beyond its reach. They are non-citizens in the host country of education, where the legal framework addresses them, in an incomplete and unsatisfactory fashion, and fails to provide adequately for their welfare. As globally mobile they tend to 'fall between the cracks' of two divergent regulatory frameworks, and in a similar manner to globally mobile workers and refugees. Here the gap in governance, the incompleteness of the fractured regulatory framework, mirrors the fractured subjectivity of the student, that sense – enforced by the way that others relate to them – that they are outsiders.

Yet the story is by no means all bad. The journey across borders is also in itself empowering, opening up new freedoms for international students, while also enriching the countries that they enter. Can global mobility become the base on which something new and positive is built? The space between recognised national borders transcends the categories of 'global' and 'local' (Sassen, 2002a, 2007a, 2007b; Krahmann, 2003; Gough, 2004; Slaughter, 2004; Swyngedouw, 2004, 2005). Larner and Walters (2004) suggest there is a need to unpack (mis)conceptions of global–local interaction by applying critical understandings of governance in international studies.

We have set out to do so in this book. But it is not enough just to state the problem in these terms. We need solutions. It is necessary to unpack the complex practical relationships between regulatory actions at the national, regional and global levels. These actions are not sequential, but simultaneous. Globalisation theory teaches us that actions at a particular place and time will have ramifications and impacts in a different place, potentially at the same and/or a different time. While not being deterministic, as Held and McGrew (2000, p 4) remind us, global studies need to capture and problematise 'the expanding scale, growing magnitude, speeding up and deepening impact of interregional flows and patterns of social interaction.'

International students are both agents and subjects in each of these spheres of intensification. Affected by everything, at the centre of the contemporary world, they are also outside it. Their rights and their sense of belonging are always in question. We argue that they will always be 'Othered', always find themselves partly outside the regulatory frame as commonly understood, unless and until they can access some form of trans-national citizenship.

Purpose and method

The central objective of this book is to critically examine the construction of international students' rights through a regulatory lens, reflecting critically on Australia and New Zealand's regulatory institutions, and associated student welfare consequences. The focus on regulation allows us to consider how the regulatory framework can be overhauled so as to improve wellbeing. The other major objective, springing directly from the first, is to suggest the kind of regulatory overhaul needed to transform the position of international students to one more consistent with a social, and not just economic, rights approach.

The book uses evidence gathered in empirical research on international education in Australia and New Zealand to analyse the impact of regulation, and the gaps it leaves. The thematic emphasis is on how these countries regulate, formally and informally, to provide for the social and economic rights of international students. Methodologically, the book uses an exploratory comparative case study research design. As noted, this also takes into account the interaction between national, trans-national and global institutions, which are refracted differently in each country. This is an idea of long standing in the international and comparative politics literature (Pierson, 1996; Weiss, 1998). For us, however, it also takes into account not only the formal institutional picture of regulation, but also informal regulation.

Each of the two national regimes is set down in a separate chapter, and then the two cases are directly compared, with the separable trans-national aspects of regulation identified and incorporated into the analysis. The use of two national cases, allowing us to explore the problem in a comparative framework, is a crucial aspect of the analysis. The comparator countries, Australia and New Zealand, are discussed with other, comparable education exporter countries in the background. The comparative approach helps to sort that which is generic to the problem of globally mobile students in nations with a commercial education export sector – and in some respects, generic to all nations providing international education – from that which is specific to Australia and New Zealand. Nationally specific problems are more easily rectified without tackling the difficult underlying issue of global mobility amid national systems. Above all the generic issues are the ones that need to be uncovered and addressed, or the problems will recur.

Following Baldwin and Cave (1999) we use 'regulation' to signify the multitude of ways in which 'rules' may be set and the conduct of regulatory agents is affected. Regulatory practices close to the subject are especially powerful. Crucially, regulation also sets rules by which the broader concept of 'governance' can be understood. The book analyses the central regulatory mechanisms which set the rules by which international students live their lives, and by which conditions are set for them, which in both cases are simultaneously national and trans-national. Regulation refers to commands and binding rules, forms of direct and deliberate influence, and '*all* forms of social control and influence' (Baldwin and Cave, 1999, p 2; emphasis added). Here, however, 'regulation' includes considerations of formal, or legal and quasi-legal, informal and often personal and interpersonal mechanisms. It touches the rewards international students reap or can reap from studying overseas, the social and economic challenges they face, and their rights and vulnerabilities in a global market and within cultures that are often foreign to them.

Thus the analysis opens up several dimensions of student life: citizenship status itself, and relationships with universities, host government departments and authorities, the general public, employers, membership-based organisations, and family and social networks. The book also discusses both the scholarly theorisations of regulation and regulatory practices. Ultimately each of these two sets of development – knowledge about regulation and the practices of regulation – feeds into the evolution of the other. Thus the book draws out the implications of its evidence for regulatory scholarship, practical regulation and ameliorative social policy.

Like the fast moving global landscape in education, the scholarship on regulation continually alters itself. The analysis explores the coverage and non-coverage of international students' rights in the social and economic spheres, typically those aspects of rights that aid assessments of citizenship status. This is not a new approach. But the discussion transcends social citizenship as it was understood in scholarly work on post-Second World War welfare states (Marshall, 1963). The global element is a vital addition. Forays into, on the one hand, the trans-national sphere, and on the other, the details of everyday life, provide different approximations of general wellbeing. Reconciling these differing notions of wellbeing is one of the unfulfilled agendas of regulation, and it is central to the mission of this book.

The book is also part of a larger discussion of regulation and governance and touches on some currents within that literature. Regulation and governance theorists demonstrate that conditions of life, and livelihoods, depend increasingly on standards set by institutions – in this case, education providers – that, while not formally under the control of the state at the national level, are instruments of governance by indirect means. This kind of indirect steering by the state, which provides more space for local initiative and semi-voluntary consent and lightens the political load associated with direct command, is increasingly central to contemporary societies (Baldwin et al, 1998; Braithwaite and Drahos, 2000; O'Brien et al, 2000; Rosenau, 2000; Black, 2002, 2003; Dawkins, 2003; Held, 2004; Braithwaite, 2006, 2008). Here universities and their students form part of a more complex picture in the determination of social and economic life conditions. The book contributes to understandings of contemporary regulation through the special case of international education.

Data sources

The empirical data were gathered through in-depth interviews with two types of informant. The first group consisted of those who knew the regulation of international education: those who designed, supervised and implemented its regulation. There were 24 interviews in this group, 13 in Australia and 11 in New Zealand, with university staff, policy personnel from the relevant civil service departments, and from a non-government international education marketing organisation in each country. University personnel were chosen on the basis that they were working within their institution's international education portfolio or office, including both senior administrative staff and international student service delivery staff in each country. Civil service employees were included because they were policy makers and/or staff responsible for the administration of the central formal regulatory instruments in each country: in Australia the Education Services for Overseas Students (ESOS) Act of 2000 (amended in 2010) and *The national code of practice for registration authorities and training to overseas students* (the 'National Code') of 2001 (revised in 2007; see AEI, 2007); in New Zealand *The code of practice for the pastoral care of international students* (the 'Pastoral Care Code') of 2002 (revised in 2010).

In the latter case a high-level employee of the IEAA, or the 'Appeal Authority', which has no equivalent in Australia, was also interviewed in order to provide data from the perspective of an organisation which has regulatory influence on student welfare but which is formally independent of the rest of the civil service, and the university system. These data are essential to studying the New Zealand system. Finally, representatives from the main international education marketing organisation in each country were interviewed, again to provide an independent voice, but one that had a different perspective to any other party within the international education sector.

The second group of interviewees, international students studying onshore in Australia and New Zealand, was significantly larger. The total was 270, although these take a somewhat secondary role in the analysis, serving mainly as statistical summaries and as a means to assess the validity of staff data. After all, staff are more instrumental given that they are regulators. As illustrated in Table 1.1, there were 200 students in Australia and 70 in New Zealand. This proportionality is broadly reflective of the size of the global market share of each nation. Australia has almost four times as many international students in higher education as New Zealand (OECD, 2011; UNESCO, 2011). Students interviewed for the study were from nine universities in Australia, from 38 on the main schedule of public higher education institutions, and two universities in New Zealand out of eight. The interviewee cohort was similarly spread in relation to student source country (see Table 1.1), with students coming from a similar range of source countries in each case, reflecting the larger student population. The main numbers were from East Asia, Southeast Asia, South Asia and Europe, with smaller numbers from North America, Latin America and Africa.

Table 1.1: Students interviewed by country of origin

Region	Number of students (Australia)	Number of students (New Zealand)
East Asia (China, Korea, Japan, Taiwan, Hong Kong)	42	27
Southeast Asia and Pacific (Indonesia, Malaysia, Singapore, Vietnam, Thailand, Laos, Burma, Philippines)	90	22
Europe (France, Germany, Sweden, Russia, Ireland)	6	11
South Asia (India, Sri Lanka, Pakistan and Nepal)	40	4
North America and Britain (US, Canada and the UK)	5	4
Other (Latin America, Middle East, Africa)	17	2
Total	**200**	**70**

All interviews were conducted face-to-face using a semi-structured interview schedule of 30-60 minutes' duration. Australian interviews commenced in 2003 and concluded in 2005 while New Zealand interviews took place in 2005 and 2006. All student interviews were only with currently enrolled students in at least their second semester of study. In most institutions staff in charge of international students arranged the interviews. University staff, themselves unconnected to the programme of staff interviews, contacted students and organised the time and venue for each interview. This ensured that no interviewees were coerced or pressured to participate. At some of the institutions international students were contacted by email, and students who were interested in participating contacted the interview coordinator. In addition, snowball sampling was used once initial contacts had been established. No interviewee is identified and neither is any institution in this book. No attempt was made for any data to be statistically representative of either student or staff experiences because the analysis is qualitative and interpretive in nature.

Structure of the book

The following chapter, Chapter Two, provides the conceptual context for the analysis. It defines 'regulation' by reviewing the literature on regulation theory alongside the allied but larger concept of governance. This is related back to international education at the national, regional, cross-national comparative and trans-national and global levels. It also locates international education within the larger edifice of higher education regulation. There is some reference to principles and factors not necessarily related to wellbeing, to provide an intellectual scaffolding for regulation, but the main purpose of the chapter is to connect regulation with student welfare.

Chapters Three and Four place Australia and New Zealand within the global market for higher education, with an emphasis on the English-speaking nations and the nations of East and Southeast Asia and the Asia-Pacific region. Chapter Three summarises the political economy of the global market as a whole, while Chapter Four closely discusses Australia and New Zealand. These chapters underpin coverage of the student welfare regimes in the two countries given in Chapters Five, Six and Seven.

Chapter Five focuses on the regulation of the welfare and agency of international students enrolled onshore in Australia. It focuses on both formal regulatory codes, and in particular the ESOS framework, which incorporates the ESOS Act and the National Code. Informal modes of regulation are also given significant attention, and the formal and informal aspects are considered in unison. Chapter Six follows the same template for New Zealand. New Zealand uses a relatively streamlined formal regulatory instrument, the Pastoral Care Code, in combination with the IEAA, which has no equivalent in the Australian regime. The chapter assesses its significance as an independent regulatory voice.

Building on the analysis of Australian and New Zealand regulation in Chapters Five and Six, Chapter Seven conducts a direct comparative analysis of the two regimes. It emphasises the ways in which each caters for the social and economic rights of international students, and addresses their advantages and shortcomings in that regard. It reveals the complex patterns of interaction between formal and informal regulation, uses the interview data to examine the regulatory instruments in the practical context of the information available (and most often not readily available) to students, and considers whether New Zealand's pastoral care approach is superior in practice to Australia's consumer protection framework.

Chapter Eight draws out larger issues, invoking national and trans-national regulatory concepts. Placing the regulatory regimes of Australia and New Zealand in the context of the whole English language group of countries and the market in Asia-Pacific, and in the light of what we know about globalisation, it summarises the central implications of the analysis for the welfare of international students, for regulation and for scholarship on regulation and social policy. Here interactions between local, national and trans-national and global support structures, formal and informal, are central to the argument. It considers how regulation might be made more conducive to international students' rights in the social and economic spheres. It then puts forward prescriptions for rendering more effective the formal regulatory regimes of Australia and New Zealand, and exporter countries like them. It finds that the key issue in redesigning regulation is to come to grips with the temporary migration status of cross-border students, and the need for a trans-national form of student citizenship. Chapter Nine closes with a summary discussion and conclusion.

TWO

Governing globalisation?
National regulation and
international student wellbeing

Introduction

Economic anthropologist Karl Polanyi (1944) argued in his *The great transformation* that not only should markets not be left alone to 'self-regulate', but that in the long term they *could not* function by themselves. If the state did not step into their operation and if other institutional forces and collectivities were not engaged for social and community enhancement, markets would not allocate resources efficiently. The market would fail comprehensively unless it was regulated by the state and influenced by non-commercially interested actors. Polanyi agreed with Robert Owen, who argued that the 'market economy if left to evolve according to its own laws would create great and permanent evils.' Focusing on both humans and nature, Polanyi (1944, p 130) saw that 'leaving the fate of soil and people to the market would be tantamount to annihilating them.' According to him, the saving grace for both the market and society was that market forces alone did not produce capitalism. The evolution of capitalist production was marked by a '*double* movement' (emphasis added):

> The one was the principle of economic liberalism, aiming at the establishment of a self-regulating market, relying on the support of the trading classes, and using largely *laissez-faire* and free trade as its methods; the other was the principle of social protection aiming at the conservation of man and nature as well as productive organisation, relying on the varying support of those most immediately affected by the deleterious action of the market – primarily, but not exclusively, the working and the landed classes – and using protective legislation, restrictive associations, and other instruments of intervention as its methods. (Polanyi, 1944, p 132)

Here Polanyi's contribution to the social science of political economy, and the analysis of global markets in particular, outlived him (North, 1977; Stanfield, 1980; Block and Somers, 1984). His ideas on market regulation had much salience in the context of financial crisis in the late 1990s (Bugra and Agartan, 2007; Harvey et al, 2007) and the deeper downturn that began in 2008 but had its roots in much earlier financial market trends (Begg, 2008; Halliday, 2008). Polanyi is also applicable to developments in the global education market. As we argue below, an understanding of regulation theory holds the key to analysing international education and to reform leading to enhanced student welfare.

In a number of ways international education is a fruitful case study of regulation itself. It highlights the complex nature of regulation in practice, and the unresolved problem of aligning national and global systems. International education regulation calls for market drivers to be balanced with social and human need. The central objective of this chapter is to situate international education within the discussion of regulation. The chapter explores the concept of regulation and the accompanying concept of governance, touching on the main analytical approaches offered in the literature. It looks at globalisation and the problem of global regulation, and also considers the legal framework governing the student experience in higher education.

The national and global dimensions of education are linked by an extensive and complex lattice of practices in trade, off-campus learning, quality assurance and migration. Although some of this runs through states and legal systems, much of it does not. This necessitates analysis not just of formal regulation of international student wellbeing, but also regulation covering the informal dimension. The concept of informal regulation springs from contemporary regulation theory and we find empirically that it pervades practice in, and the analysis of, the Australian and New Zealand contexts, and it is important in the analysis of them.

In international education the global dimension of regulation is embryonic, the national/global link is poorly developed and there is little formal encouragement for ensuring students' wellbeing as a global matter. Despite little systematic analysis in the scholarly literature, as noted in Chapter One and in Marginson et al (2010), what we do know suggests that existing government policies cover student welfare in a patchy fashion. In the commercial export nations of Australia, New Zealand and the UK there are few mandated minimum standards of welfare, aside from consumer protection provisions. In most other nations even a consumer protection framework has been little developed. The lacunae in formal regulation make the informal dimension even more important than they already, always are. Nevertheless, while informal welfare can be vital to both daily security and a richer overall experience, informal regulation does not wholly substitute for a formal regulatory regime.

The most potent context of international education is the competition for shares within the global market. The drivers have been mainly although not solely located in the market; more specifically, the economics of education trade (Hira, 2003; Bashir, 2007). Given Polanyi's point about the need for regulation and civil order to balance market forces, it is unsurprising that the dominance of the market is associated with the social vulnerabilities of students. Much cross-border activity in higher education is regulated by 'push' and 'pull' forces in trade, expressed mainly through student country-destination choice and movement between exporter and importer nations (Mazzarol and Soutar, 2002; OECD, 2004a). Welfare-related issues, such as personal safety, health provisions and access to paid part-time employment, do factor into student choice, yet they are all but missing in national and trans-national policy and regulatory responses.

Between them national governments and global intergovernmental organisations have the means to provide comprehensively for student welfare. Formal regulation could be designed so as to mandate student rights and resources on a universal basis, providing protection and sustaining active agency. Formal regulation would thereby buttress the contribution of informal regulation, as well as holding out a safety net partially compensating those students for whom informal supports are weak or absent, including students in isolated non-urban locations and students from home countries with few social connections in the country of education. But the constructive potentials of regulation remain largely unrealised and the political will is all but absent.

Having said that, the state of play in regulation theory provides a vital thoroughfare to understanding student wellbeing.

Ideas about regulation

In traditional public administration parlance, regulation was conceived as 'a mode of governmental activity' that was 'identifiable and discrete' (Baldwin and Cave, 1999, p 2). The nation-state was at the centre of public affairs, issuing legal and normative rules and standards. Subjects had to comply or face penalties or disincentives. This is the basis of the 'command and control' administrative model, largely consistent with ideas associated with economic sociologist Max Weber (1921, 1947). In the last two decades, however, understandings of regulation have become broader, shadowing developments in regulatory practice. In an era of marketisation of governmental functions and the use of regulated markets as a policy tool, and partial decentralisation of policy and devolution of state responsibilities (see, for example, Le Grand and Bartlett, 1993; Powell, 2007), traditional state regulation is still relevant but it is not the entire picture. There are more mixed, complex, diffuse and fragmented governance and regulation, and there are more concepts to unpack.

International education is an exemplar of these broader trends in government and a fitting subject for the application of recent regulation concepts. With regulation in practice having been re-ordered so as to invoke a plurality of legal and policy domains, this has prompted the need for interdisciplinarity in scholarship (Parker et al, 2004; Arup et al, 2006), an approach which we follow. Correspondingly, it is now common to view the concept of regulation as being multidirectional and multidimensional in character, with some noting that it has been 'globalised' (Braithwaite and Drahos, 2000; Drahos and Braithwaite, 2001). Above all regulation has been 'decentred', with some of the responsibilities of the state having been devolved to actors in the market and in civil society. Even two decades ago Ayres and Braithwaite (1992) made the point that regulation was or should be increasingly 'responsive', implying that the state was proactive but also *reactive* and acting in new contexts as part of a larger network of institutional actors, subjects and relations (Braithwaite, 2006, p 886). 'Self-regulation', whether voluntary, coerced or forced, is also more common and more significant for policy makers and analysts in most areas of economic activity (Baldwin and Cave, 1999, pp 125-37), including international education.

Governance and regulation

An important relationship is that between governance and regulation. Developments in the regulation of international education are captured by both terms, although the main focus of this book is regulation.

Governance is broader and more encompassing than its counterpart. Braithwaite and colleagues (2007), consistent with Black (2002), argue:

> Governments and governance are about providing, distributing, and regulating. Regulation [on the other hand] can be conceived as that large subset of governance that is about steering the flow of events and behaviour, as opposed to providing and distributing. (Braithwaite et al, 2007, p 3)

Parker and Braithwaite (2003, p 119) argue that governance necessarily involves a multilevel analysis, with 'a progressively narrowing focus, like a set of Russian dolls, from "intergovernmental studies", to whole of government studies, to studies of legislatures ... and so on.' This idea is suggestive for our analysis, as indicated in the final section of this chapter. Frederickson (2005, p 283) adds that governance includes within its ambit the 'contextual influences that shape the practices of public administration.' Governance includes 'inter-jurisdictional relations and third party implementation of public administration', and 'the influence or power of non-state and non-jurisdictional public collectives.' The concept embraces national and local institutions such as governments and public bureaucracies, education systems, economic systems and business organisations, and less formal entities such as communities and the family (Rosenau, 2000, p 181; King and Schneider, 1991, pp 181-2). Taken in these more liberal, somewhat fractured interpretations governance approximates French philosopher and social theorist Michel Foucault's (1977-78/2007, Lecture Four) notion, not of government or regulation, but of 'governmentality'.

In our domain the global dimension is important. 'Global governance' refers to the ways that institutions, organisations and individuals interact to formulate social and economic conditions at the global level. This takes in formal global entities of the kind found in 'global social policy' (Deacon with Hulse and Stubbs, 1997; Yeates, 2001, 2008; Deacon, 2007) while also prescribing a central place for multinational corporations and other organisations whose missions may be neither social in orientation nor geared toward humanistic ends (see, for example, Dawkins, 2003; Held, 2004). Higher education providers are multinational, revenue-raising organisations that in relation to international education particularly, are important actors in global governance (Ramia et al, 2011).

Like Baldwin and Cave (1999), Arup and colleagues (2006) and others, we define *regulation* as the multitude of mechanisms – formal and legal, informal and interpersonal – which set social and economic rules, norms and customs. According to the editors of the journal *Regulation and Governance* (Braithwaite et al, 2007), the contemporary concept of regulation has long and multidisciplinary roots (see also the authoritative surveys of the regulation concept in Baldwin et al, 1998; Baldwin and Cave, 1999, Chapter 3; Parker et al, 2004; Arup et al, 2006). Braithwaite et al (2007) note that one branch is the work of US scholars who interrogated government and industry institutions in the Progressive Era of the late 19th and early 20th centuries. Another branch is the movement from the 1970s onwards toward more formal regulation of facets of social and economic life including consumer and civil rights, health and safety and the natural environment. The formation of the EU later enhanced interest in trans-national competition and cooperation and social policy questions. Corporate and political crime have inspired further work, as has the fusion of law and economics, most influentially in the 1980s Thatcher regime in the UK and 'Reaganomics' in the US. Further still, economic and business history also spawned regulatory ideas, inspiring the sub-field of neo-institutional economics in particular.

If 'regulation' is taken to encompass more than that which professional regulators do, regulation is inevitable, pervasive and inescapable. It comes in many forms and most often has unexpected or less easily recognised sources. This is the case particularly in relation to people such as international students, whose lives are affected by factors that do not neatly fit within the confines of state-based or national public policies and that are shaped strongly by less understood regulatory forces such as family and social networks, not to mention international organisations in the intergovernmental and non-government sectors.

In the context of global market forces but in the realm of the personal and interpersonal, informal regulatory context, the wellbeing of international students is partially – indeed as we find here, predominantly – a process of self-regulation. Students' own agency is vital. It is, as the famous welfare theorists Nussbaum and Sen (1993) argue, a process of harnessing one's own 'capabilities' as the principal road to greater opportunity (see also Marginson, 2011b). Individual agency is not merely an individual question, however, and indeed students do belong to and act as collectivities, and collective action matters to their social, economic and political status as a movement (Sebastien, 2009).

Our interviews with international students, university staff and regulators/policy makers, analysed in Chapters Five, Six and Seven, highlight the role of the informal domain. Both the formal and informal domains are incomplete and imperfect, and one is not a substitute for the other. In line with Parker and colleagues (2004), we reflect on the questions of 'intent' and 'agency' in international education. We simultaneously consider the regulatory impact of both private and public intent, as these become manifest in both public settings and social and private networks. In the sense of Parker and colleagues we consider 'intended agency' alongside 'the unintended effects of that agency'.

Formal regulation and law

Within the formal domain of regulation some scholars take the law as their starting point (Black, 2002; Parker et al, 2004; Arup et al, 2006). Regulation theory prescribes that practising lawyers and legal scholars must grapple with the interaction between law and non-legal phenomena, and with policy, markets and the rules set by civil society institutions. The resultant picture is complex. As Black (2001, p 14) reminds us, the analyst of regulation must account for:

> ... the legal framework, the characterisation of the regulatees, the relational distance between regulator and regulatee, the type of firm [or other organisational context], the nature of the [regulatory] breach, organisational structures and norms, personal backgrounds and attitudes, and the broader political, social and moral context in which the regulation sits.

Agency is mediated by regulation and in some instances most clearly by law. Law is a key arm of the trans-disciplinary field that is international education regulation. Conceiving regulation as encompassing standard-setting and the mechanisms used for the compliance and monitoring of standards, Parker and colleagues (2004) highlight three ways that regulation theory engages legal practitioners and scholars in issues and concepts within and outside the law as traditionally defined. First, the regulation perspective involves dialogue between lawyers and regulationists. Second, regulation studies consider the different purposes and orientations of various areas of the law and the interconnections and contests between them. Third, being part of regulatory theory, legal scholarship focuses on the ways that law interacts with other forms of regulation. These three elements are all relevant for the analysis of regulation in international education in light of the interviews with students, academic staff and policy officers. The argument of Parker and colleagues suggests the need for more meaningful dialogue between lawyers and the broader regulatory community, and between legal and regulation scholars (see Parker et al, 2004), in international education and other regulatory domains. This would correspond to growing real-world interaction within and between different areas of the law, and between law and official and unofficial standard-setting processes in most aspects of social and economic life.

The most important starting point for understanding international education regulation is the law at the level of the nation-state. This is borne out in our empirical analysis, mainly Chapters Five and Six.

National regulatory context

Rules based on the nation-state, legal frameworks and customs relating to student welfare tend to be patchy in the sense that they result from a combination of global and national influences, mostly market-related and consumer protection-oriented. Often they bear little or no relationship to phenomena outside their own borders; in other respects, the various national systems move in parallel, through a process of voluntary cross-border imitation; while a third kind of phenomena are fostered by global agencies, deliberate cross-border agreements and other processes originating from outside the national regulatory context. This makes it important to consider both the global origin phenomena and to apply comparative analysis to each specific national regulatory system. We begin, however, by considering the national context in stand-alone terms.

Legal provisions

National legal regimes conform predominantly to one or other of the common law or 'civil law' traditions (Lloyd, 1981, pp 222-4). National higher education institutions and systems in once-colonised countries, as with their institutions in general, bear the hallmarks of the imperial powers that controlled them (Altbach, 2007, Chapter 9). Australia and New Zealand, the two countries that constitute the focus of empirical analysis in this book, share adherence to the British tradition of 'common law' or judge-made law. Such legal systems also exist in many other former British colonies, including Canada and the US. In Asia there is India, Malaysia and Singapore. Civil law countries, mainly those of Western Europe which have older, Roman-based legal systems, are characterised first and foremost by reliance on academic-influenced legislation rather than cases overseen by judges, and juries in criminal cases. Law in such a system is more firmly based on the morals that predominate in the wider national society.

Asian countries that have civil law systems, most of which are among the major importers of international education and thus are sources of students to English-speaking common law countries, were historically colonies of European powers, and especially those of the French and the Dutch. These countries include Vietnam, Cambodia and Indonesia.

Other countries were influenced by the European traditions without having been formally colonised. This group includes China, Japan, South Korea and Thailand. In contrast, the legal systems of common law Asian countries are more directly exposed to English traditions including Protestantism, secularism and empiricism. Like the British group these countries also see law making largely as a process reflecting custom and practice, applied 'commonly' within the country, handed down mainly by judges who rely on the doctrine of 'precedent', and relying on a hierarchy of courts as well as juries for criminal cases. Common law systems also rely on legislation, increasingly so, giving some cause to argue that the distinction between the two kinds of legal systems is breaking down (Fordham, 2006; cf Zaphiriou, 1994). Yet primacy in common law is still given to case-by-case legal development.

In higher education, notwithstanding debate on whether 'legalism' in the form of legislation is currently excessive and whether a culture emphasising interpretation by and within higher education institutions is more appropriate (Bergan, 2004), the relevant bodies of law within common law countries are best understood as combinations of cases, legislation and legal and pseudo-legal tribunals. Despite the primacy of case law in common law countries, the regime of regulation in higher education is arguably not best captured by cases. Higher education institutions are administered more by regulations and via 'management' and 'enterprise' (Marginson and Considine, 2000; Peters, 2007, Chapter 3). Little of the regulation of higher education, formal and informal, is captured in the narratives of court and tribunal systems. At the same time, law is increasingly important because of the growing culture of litigation in the sector (Poskanzer, 2002; Astor, 2005; Olliffe and Stuhmcke, 2007).

There are few comprehensive texts on higher education law. Farrington and Palfreyman's (2006) *The law of higher education* covers issues as diverse as the legal status of higher education institutions; the roles of government, research and teaching funding councils and quality assurance agencies; and the impact of EU law and international obligations in higher education, to which this chapter turns later (Farrington and Palfreyman, 2006, Section I, Chapters 2-4). Under higher education, governance and management are matters of: the question of 'officers' versus 'managers'; charity trusteeship and personal liberty on and around campuses; law in relation to academic and educational meetings; and student unions (Section II, Chapters 5-9). The law covering staff and students includes the higher education employment contract for academics and the statutory regulation of employment; dismissal and disputes; the legal relationship between students and the institution in which they are enrolled; the status of students as consumers; and the role of judicial review in higher education institutions (Section III, Chapters 10-15).

Within the realm of academic issues are included: academic freedom, intellectual property and in particular its ownership and exploitation, and data protection and freedom of information (Section IV, Chapters 16-18). Given that contemporary higher education is a business, the law must incorporate universities as trading companies, and given the need to compete both locally and globally, many institutions engage in mergers and acquisitions and other commercial agreements (Section V, Chapters 19-21). The allied matters of property and estate are also on the rise, including dealings involving campus security, land occupiers' liability, issues of accessibility for staff and students with disabilities. Student housing is increasingly important (Section VI, Chapters 22-25), as is health and safety. Risk assessment, institutions' preventative strategies and dispute settlements are also prominent (Section VII, Chapters 26-27). Finally, it is noteworthy that all of these areas exist partially in their comparative context, and so in law, as in other areas of regulation examined here, analysis of cross-national similarities and differences, and the political and institutional sources and significance of these, are part of higher education law (Section VIII, Chapters 28-30).

A survey of the law in the US, as provided in key texts such as Kaplan and Lee's (2006) now two-volume *The law of higher education*, reveals more richness than the UK. In addition to the issues covered in the case of the UK, with the US being a federal country, its law also covers more sources of formal regulation including: federal and state constitutions; state common law; more relevant foreign and international laws; issues relating to the public–private institutional dichotomy; a greater role for religion in higher education, given the greater number of faith-based institutions than in the UK; and the relationship between law and policy (Volume 1, Part 1, Section 1), as often discussed by regulation theorists. Alternative dispute resolution methods such as mediation, conciliation and arbitration play a greater role in the US (Part 1, Section 2.3). Questions of authority involve greater recourse to the law of tort liability (Part 2, Section 3.3), and many more provisions are in place to govern industrial and workplace relations, including collective bargaining (Part 2, Sections 4.3, 4.5-4.6), given that higher education providers are also employers.

Individual student rights and responsibilities are more extensive and more specific in the US than in the UK, as are rules covering student organisations and their membership. This includes not merely student faith-based and activity-based non-governmental organisations (NGOs), but also fraternities and sororities, student press organisations, and athletics teams and clubs (Volume II, Part 4, Sections 9-10). Relationships between higher education institutions and education associations, business and industry bodies, and state and local communities, are also prominent (Part 6, Sections 14-15). In the US students are recognised under the Constitution as legal 'persons' and thus have their own body of enforceable rights under federal statutes (Kaplan and Lee, 2006, pp 54-7). The age of majority – and with it rights and responsibilities of students – varies with different branches of law and among different states (Section 8.1.2).

Rights under contract may be affected. Common examples of welfare-related areas in contracts between higher education institutions and their students include housing, if the institution provides it, campus-based food service contracts and loan agreements. The student catalogue or handbook is increasingly being seen as a contract. Contracts may be 'express' or 'implied', meaning that terms and conditions do not need to be in writing to be enforceable. Academic and disciplinary disputes are also covered under contract law (see Section 8.1.3). Students also have rights to their academic freedom, although these are not as extensively regulated as those of staff, borrowing instead from the German university tradition of the freedom to learn, or *Lernfreiheit* (Section 8.1.4). Provisions also exist to protect student rights on matters of admission (Section 8.2.1).

Discrimination against, and affirmative action for, students are covered under law, including questions of 'race', sex, disability, age and residence and immigration status (Sections 8.2.4.1-8.2.4.6). International students, as 'temporary or non-immigrant aliens', have less law covering them than 'resident aliens', the former implying student visa holders and the latter those who are not citizens but who hold permanent resident status. After 9/11 there have been greater levels of government discretion as to acceptance and rejection of entry visa for students from Muslim and Arab parts of the world (Urias and Yeakey, 2009).

Principles governing student financial aid are covered mainly in contract law, whether these relate to awards in the form of scholarships, assistantships, loans, fellowships or preferential tuition rates (Section 8.3). Complications and more sources of law apply in relation to non-financial terms and conditions such as those relating to discrimination (Sections 8.3.3, 8.3.5) or affirmative action (Section 8.3.4) or to duties on the part of a student to perform instructional or laboratory work, to play on a university sporting team or to provide other services (Section 8.3.1). On the matter of campus security, although there is no specified responsibility on the part of institutions to provide for student safety

(Section 3.3.2), some institutions have been found liable in legal actions taken by students, when injuries were foreseeable or the campus had a history of criminal activity (Section 8.6.1). Consequences vary if, for example, an attacker was a student or a campus intruder (Section 8.6.2) – the duty of the institution being stronger in the latter case than in the former – and outside of the contractual realm a number of state and federal statutes and statutory changes apply (Section 8.6.3).

In addition to financial aid and campus security, higher education institutions provide other welfare-related support services, including health services, auxiliary services for students with disabilities and services in childcare and legal assistance (Sections 8.7.2-8.7.3, 8.7.5-8.7.6). Others include academic and career counselling, placement services, resident life programming, entertainment and recreational services, parking, food and beverage and a range of other convenience-related services (Section 15.3.1). Some services are provided directly by an institution's staff and others by contracted third parties or by student groups subsidised by the institution (Sections 10.1.3, 15.2.2, 15.3.1). Funding may come from a variety of sources, including the institutions' regular budget or earmarked funds, from student tuition and other fees and from charges for the service, and from governmental, non-governmental or corporate sources. Students' rights and duties in relation to all services raise individual authority and legality issues (covered in Section 8.7).

Legal frameworks and student welfare

A sole focus on individual legal provisions such as those discussed above reveals little about broader frameworks that cover a range of issues in the one legal instrument. In higher education this translates as specific statutes or acts of Parliament covering student welfare-related provisions. In such a picture the UK appears significantly more welfare-attentive than the US, given that, like New Zealand, the UK has an independent tribunal that adjudicates on student matters that are not resolved by the higher education provider to the satisfaction of the student. Within the ambit of the Office of the Independent Adjudicator for Higher Education (OIA), as it is called, are international student matters, including welfare issues.

Taking the US situation first, although international students have access to most of the support services available to locals, few services are mandated specifically for them at the national level. Indeed it is noteworthy that despite extensive regulations governing international students' lives, few pertain to services and most relate to post-9/11 national security concerns and institutions' and students' information management and reporting requirements. Contrary to Australia and New Zealand, as discussed in Chapters Five and Six, there is no all-encompassing legal regulatory framework in the US to rival the ESOS Act and the Australian National Code, or New Zealand's Pastoral Care Code and IEAA processes. Instead, the immigration status of students is a focal point, which, once established, is relevant when students are employed part time (Section 4.6.5) and in matters of admission and tuition (Sections 8.2.4.6, 8.3.6). Immigration status also defines the kind of visa on which foreign nationals reside in the US as international students, with those solely and temporarily in the country for study purposes being labelled 'F-1s' (Section 8.7.4), or international students as defined here and in general parlance.

The Department of State has the power to grant and to deny visa status, while the Department of Homeland Security's Bureau of Citizenship and Immigration Services (CIS) has the authority to approve the institution that students may attend. CIS also monitors student academic progress and may cancel visas on the basis of poor academic performance. In addition, the Department of Homeland Security's Bureau of Immigration and Customs Enforcement (ICE) operates the Student and Exchange Visitors' Information System (SEVIS). Institutions must use SEVIS to enter and update information on every student on a student visa. Guidance for staff engaged by institutions to interpret and administer international education regulations is provided in the Association of International Educators' *Adviser's manual of federal regulations affecting foreign students and scholars* (see NAFSA, 2009).

The UK regime is in most ways and for this discussion either comparable or similar, particularly in terms of the relationship between the higher education institution and the student, and the welfare-related services provided to international students (Farrington and Palfreyman, 2006, Chapter 13). Importantly, however, in terms of student rights the UK has an additional institution, which, given the character of the New Zealand regime, is comparable with and discussed further in the New Zealand Chapter Six.

For the purpose of the current discussion, however, it is noteworthy that the UK's OIA operates under Part 2, Section 20 of the Higher Education Act 2004 in England and Wales (Olliffe and Stuhmcke, 2007). The OIA is a specialist higher education tribunal that hears cases of complaint by students and hands down binding decisions on both student and provider. In this and other ways it is based on the model of ombudsmen as first formulated in Scandinavia (Astor, 2005).

Welfare-related issues are heard and dealt with on a compulsory basis. Matters of admissions are excluded and subject instead to the courts system. Issues included within the OIA's ambit, in order of frequency in absolute numbers in 2008, for example, were: academic status (582); service issues (130); academic misconduct including plagiarism and cheating (69); discrimination and human rights (53); financial (31); other (22); and welfare and accommodation (13). Finally, the OIA hears cases on a non-discriminatory basis from students local and international alike (OIA, 2009, pp 40, 44).

Globalisation and comparativism in regulation

As we have seen, despite the centrality of the national dimension in law, student lives have trans-national dimensions, and increasingly so. Even formal national regulation that has been wholly framed within the traditions of one state, without reference to practices elsewhere, or global regulatory agents, can have trans-national implications. Moreover, through regulatory instruments, global trends are transmitted back into higher education agendas and influence the status, strategies and everyday operation of tertiary education providers (see, for example, Marginson and Rhoades, 2002; Apple et al, 2005; Mok, 2006, Chapter 1; Altbach, 2007; Peters, 2007; Scott and Dixon, 2008). As noted, some national higher education systems have enriched themselves by becoming education exporters. Everywhere research-intensive universities focus on lifting their international profiles, some by expanding the volume of international education, all via research, and moving up global rankings lists (Marginson, 2004, 2005). There has been major growth in the provision of trans-national higher education (TNHE), that is, education services that cross borders through franchising, twinning degrees, programme articulation, branch campuses and virtual and distance-based teaching and learning, and programmes delivered within corporations (McBurnie and Ziguras, 2007; Naidoo, 2009).

Regulation of international education, as for other spheres of global–national interaction, reflects 'the expanding scale, growing magnitude, speeding up and deepening impact of interregional flows and patterns of social, interaction' (Held and McGrew, 2000, p 4). International students are both agents and subjects of each of these dimensions of intensification. The lives of international students are touched simultaneously by rules and customs in local, national and global spaces. Marginson (2004) combines the three dimensions, although not in relation to student welfare, arguing for a framework using a 'glonacal' heuristic (see also Marginson and Rhoades, 2002) and combining the cross-national comparative and the global (Marginson and Mollis, 2000). This is directly applicable to the regulation of higher education in general, including student lives, in that the instruments in each space are interrelated. But overt welfare considerations are more prominent in national rules than in the global sphere, and the welfare-related regulations of nation-states do not connect effectively with international instruments.

Overemphasising the duality of the global and national categories carries the risk of portraying all nations as equal and all higher education institutions as possessing equivalent status. Formal national sovereignty might be equal in the legal and normative political and legal sense, but actual powers and resources are not equivalent. This highlights the insights offered by the comparative approach, which allows us to explore not just similarity in the national responses to universal global pressures, but also cross-national differences. Comparativism acknowledges that nations, and education providers, face global regulation from unequal and non-equivalent positions. Many countries struggle in the quest to balance national imperatives with global pressures to conform. Stronger nations can afford to be more robust and even resistant to global systems and pressures, but often the nation-state is itself the vehicle whereby global imperatives become translated into effects within higher education. For example, in South Africa, a middle-income country with more highly rated universities than any other in the African region, university leaders and system managers face trade-offs between university independence and state direction designed to achieve national trade and economic development objectives that have been framed within the global competition setting (Moja et al, 1996; Bitzer, 2002).

At the most basic level some countries are net exporters and some are net importers. Whichever is the case, however, they can and do pursue the internationalisation of education with varying national policy agendas in mind. In contrast to some comparativists who stress intraregional country similarities (Mok, 2006), McBurnie and Ziguras (2001) argue in their comparison of higher education in Hong Kong, Malaysia and Australia that national policy can and does vary according to the central rationale of the national regime. They find that Hong Kong is most motivated by a consumer protection rationale. Malaysian authorities mainly see cross-border education as a means of advancing nationalist goals, including the building of a local education infrastructure, and the preservation of Islamic values and identity. On the other hand, Australia is mainly concerned with protecting its local system and the nation's reputation as an education provider.

Thus, despite the growing international trade in education, and notwithstanding ongoing scholarly debate on the implications of globalisation for higher education regulation (Teichler, 1999; Hodson and Thomas, 2001; Mok, 2003; Angus, 2004; Enders, 2004), the governing rules and norms – formal, informal, self-formed, private and public – still have their centre of gravity at the level of the nation-state. Patterns vary across nations and regions, partly depending on whether the country is predominantly importing or exporting (Ziguras, 2003). Patterns also vary with the stage of economic development of the country or region (Bashir, 2007, pp 74-82).

Trade, trans-national education, migration and quality assurance

The most significant global initiative in the regulation of education has been the involvement of the World Trade Organization (WTO). In 1995 the WTO introduced its General Agreement on Trade in Services (GATS), a multilateral agreement to liberalise the provision of services across borders within the (now) 153 country membership. As outlined in Table 2.1 (p 36), GATS allows for four 'modes of supply': first, 'cross-border delivery' of education services, whereby services are delivered by distance in tele-education, education-testing services and education via the internet; second, 'consumption abroad', which covers students physically moving from one country to another to conduct their studies; third, 'commercial presence', including course offerings abroad through branch campuses, franchises or other provider subsidiary arrangements; and fourth, 'presence of natural persons', which covers temporary movement of teachers, lecturers and other education personnel across borders (see also Ziguras, 2003; OECD, 2004a, pp 33-7).

In the sense that TNHE is encouraged and facilitated by international institutions such as the WTO, global regulation is pushed onto nation-states 'from above', to use the terminology of Apple and colleagues (2005). Yet in the sense that higher education providers respond by increasing TNHE initiatives, regulation is also reciprocally driven 'from below', and the national context itself remains central.

GATS stands to benefit developed countries, which are typically net education exporters, at the expense of developing nations, which are typically net importers. Developing countries have excess demand, an undersupply of local education provision, while the richer exporting countries can expand capacity to service that need through cross-border education. Incentives for 'progressive liberalisation', in the terminology of GATS, are therefore significant. Hypothetically GATS has the potential to take on a major global regulatory influence through its provisions on cross-border activity. We note here that in principle GATS could insert social clauses, such that, for example, free trade in education is subject to minimum welfare standards. This is not on the agenda. It looks more unlikely over time, given that GATS has had only a modest impact. Most nations have been unwilling to sign up to genuine and extensive commitments in principle, let alone implement them (Sauvé, 2002; Knight, 2004; Ziguras, 2005; Bashir, 2007; Varghese, 2007).

In addition, member nations can weaken the effects of GATS in several ways. They can decline to make any commitments. They can qualify their commitments in a particular sector or sub-sector, choosing to continue (in WTO parlance) 'discriminatory' treatment of fellow member nations, such that some countries have made minimal commitments in the higher education sector, even if they have done more in other sectors. Alternatively countries can apply a range of limitations to all services, such as (under GATS Article XII) restrictions to 'safeguard' their 'balance of payments' if they deem GATS provisions detrimental in that regard. They can also invoke various general exceptions (under Article XIV) to amend their conditions of acceptance of GATS prescriptions. Finally, a country can withdraw from GATS and the WTO (Sauvé, 2002, pp 11-12). So far this has not happened. Countries mostly queue to join the WTO-GATS rather than seeking to leave. This has maintained the universality of the trade dimension of higher education despite its modest achievements.

Another nationally common (although in this case, not universal) approach to global phenomena is the use of international education as a medium of skilled migration. This in turn leads to national exposure to perceived or actual risk in relation to the language proficiency of student migrants. This issue has generated an especially lively debate in Australia and New Zealand (Mills et al, 2005; Ziguras and Law, 2006; Baas, 2007; Bond et al, 2007; Rodan, 2009).

Partly through GATS, but largely through an opening of global markets that would arguably have occurred in the absence of WTO-GATS, distance and off-campus delivery (GATS Mode of Supply 1), and cross-border branch campus delivery and franchise and twinning arrangements (GATS Mode of Supply 3), have increasingly been facilitated (McBurnie and Ziguras, 2001, 2007; Naidoo, 2009). This growth of TNHE has raised a number of regulatory questions. First, whereas domestic providers in importer countries are subject to all relevant national laws and formal regulations, foreign providers, providing through any of the means mentioned above, for the most

Table 2.1: Modes of supply of services under GATS

GATS mode of supply	Description	Examples for higher education
Mode 1: Cross-border delivery	Delivery of education services from exporting country A to importing country B	Distance education, tele-education, education-testing services, education via internet
Mode 2: Consumption abroad	Movement of students from importing country B to exporting country A to obtain education services	Chinese students studying in US universities, in the US
Mode 3: Commercial presence	Establishment of local unit of institution from exporting country A to importing country B	Country A's course offerings through branch campuses or subsidiaries of institutions, franchising, twinning/ articulated arrangements, etc
Mode 4: Presence of natural persons	Temporary movement of teachers, lecturers and education personnel from country A to country B to provide education services	Teacher/lecturer exchange programmes

Source: Bashir (2007) © The World Bank

part are not. Second, whereas cross-border providers are subject to the laws and regulations of their home country, many of these regulations can either be bypassed or diluted in the process of internationalising. As McBurnie and Ziguras (2001, 2007) make clear, higher education providers from developed countries can bypass their own local regulations when developing, pricing and marketing programmes to students residing in countries with less restrictive stipulations about quality.

A key problem here is that there are significant weaknesses in the concept and application of quality and quality assurance (Daniel, 2002; IAU, 2002; Uvalic-Trumbic, 2002; van Damme, 2002). In an increasingly trade-oriented and trade-reliant global higher education system, new and emerging regimes of quality are required. New forms have emerged, national and international. Are they adequate? Given that education increasingly crosses borders in response to trade, how do providers ensure that the quality of the education product is provided without compromising standards? Van Damme (2002) suggests four possible models for regulating standards. The first model would see efforts to increase international cooperation such that there would be some convergence on the standards issues seen as most important. The second would involve the upgrading of international networking and exchanges in arrangements such as cross-border quality assessment projects. A third would develop validation and meta-accreditation of quality assurance systems and agencies. Finally, a fourth model would involve the creation of a fully-fledged international agency for overseeing global quality assurance. Each model has advantages and disadvantages. To the extent that bypassing and dilution of quality occurs, both quality assurance and TNHE lead to interconnected gaps and challenges. Even where capacity needs are met, quality may be jeopardised.

Conclusion: the role of global social policy

Any picture of regulation designed to explore international student wellbeing must capture the national, trans-national and global elements of regulation. National borders have been opened up, and global–national interaction has become more prominent in the formal arena, principally by the inclusion of education within the WTO's GATS framework. This and other global pressures may encourage (or partly coerce) some nations to compromise on national policy objectives, for example, by allowing trans-national providers from the developed world to enter, virtually or through foreign direct investment, or through trans-national distance or off-campus learning, offshore campuses in host countries and cross-border franchise delivery. Nevertheless, most student mobility is in the other direction, in the temporary physical relocation of students to study in exporter countries. Mobility in either direction opens up the potential for regulation at both ends of the student geographic transfer, but significantly, the bulk of the detailed regulation takes place where the education provider is located. In cases where the provider and student are split, such as in distance education, governance is more effective at the point of production than at the point of consumption. This is symptomatic of an industry and a form of commercial globalisation in which the driver is the need of institutions for market revenues, rather than the social and educational needs of students – that is, unless regulation is modified so as to balance the dynamics of the market with social and human objectives, in the manner suggested by Polanyi.

It is striking, however, that so far not much of the growth in formal regulation has been directed to student wellbeing, as distinct from the facilitation of trade in their education. Yet it would be a mistake to overlook the welfare-relevant instruments that exist in various national jurisdictions and in the international and trans-national spheres. Understanding these instruments is a vital prerequisite to reforming welfare, the task we undertake in Chapter Eight. At the same time, consistent with regulation theory, informal regulation is part of the story. Welfare regulation is shaped, on the one hand, by the interaction between formal and informal regulation, and on the other, by the interface between the national and global dimensions of regulation. Regulation processes take place within the larger interaction between regulation and governance. Relations between governance and regulation are key to understanding the role of institutional development at the interface between global social policy and global social regulation, the focus of a new sub-field within the literature.

Deacon (2007, p 1) conceives the synthesis of global social policy and global regulation in terms of two central phenomena. First, 'the social policy prescriptions for national social policy being articulated by global actors', principally the UN and various of its social and human development agencies, The World Bank, the International Monetary Fund and international NGOs in fields such as human development and other trans-national social issues. Second, 'the emerging supranational social policies and mechanisms of global redistribution, global social regulation and global social rights' (see also Deacon, 1997; Yeates, 2001, 2008). Prior to the preparation for this book, international education had not been extensively interrogated using this framework, nor had international students featured as its analytical subjects.

The wellbeing of international students is first and foremost a social policy question. This chapter suggests that social policy must be infused with global regulation and governance to be maximally useful. For global social policy adherents, questions of social citizenship are writ global, albeit that the pathways from global to national and back again are not always entirely clear. We trust that our analysis of the regulation of international students in Australia and New Zealand, while comparing the two national settings with each other and locating them in a broader international context, and considering both formal and informal regulation, will enable readers to consider the need for and potentialities of the global social regulation of student welfare.

THREE

Fast growing, diverse: mapping the business of international education

Introduction

Understanding the wellbeing of international students requires a discussion of the global market context within which cross-border education is taking place. At the heart of the international education strategies of many exporter governments is the ongoing competitive push for global market share. Australia and New Zealand typify this export-maximising approach, as we argue in the coming chapters. Before embarking on an analysis of these two countries, however, it is important to survey the political economy of the global market within which nation-states are competing, and this is the central purpose of this chapter.

The international education market is fast growing and diverse, in terms of the source countries of students, in the provider nations that provide educational services, in the types of institutional provider and in the fields and levels of study, and in the modes of delivery of cross-border degrees. Primary national motives behind international education range from profit making to foreign aid, with a variety of provision in between that combines subsidised cultural mixing and part self-financed career development. Different nations favour different approaches, and these embody a variety of policy objectives and cultural educational traditions. Economic and cultural globalisation in an unequal world are manifest in the growing role of global business and global English; in the larger changes to regulatory and institutional structures and arrangements; in the increased impact of time–space compression; and in the global map of options now facing millions of students and educators. The increasingly global character of tertiary education activities is creating more pressure on the regulatory systems that continue to be largely national in form (Marginson, 2011a).

The first section of this chapter provides an overview of the global student market through the lens of student mobility. It includes discussion of the market factors that drive mobility, the political economy of the education export industry and the special case of doctoral education, which does not usually attract fees but is instead subsidised mainly by scholarship support. The next two sections discuss the market position of, and the key trends engaging, the main English-speaking export countries that are competing with Australia and New Zealand for market share. Respectively, these are the US, Canada and the UK. The fourth and final section discusses the Asia–Pacific region. Together the Anglophone and Asia-Pacific countries constitute two divergent but important 'slices' of the global market with close relevance to international education in Australia and New Zealand.

Global student mobility

The Organisation for Economic Co-operation and Development (OECD) distinguishes between data on 'international students', those who cross borders for education and are thus part of the global market, and data on 'foreign students', which also includes resident non-citizens. The second category can include students from families resident in the country for several generations but not yet granted citizenship. The first set of data is preferred for analytical purposes, but as yet some nations provide data only on foreign students. These include France, Germany and Canada, all of which are among the world's top exporters (OECD, 2011, pp 364-5). Thus the only comprehensive picture of the global market uses the foreign student data and tends to exaggerate the role of nations that are slow to turn residents into citizens.

In 1975 the number of foreign students was just 0.8 million. In 2010, the most recent year on which statistics are available, it was 4.1 million. It more than quadrupled in little more than a generation. Between 2000 and 2010 the total number of foreign students – those studying outside their countries of citizenship for one year or more – increased by 99 per cent, starting at 2.1 million and growing at an average of 7.1 per cent per annum. Approximately 77 per cent of the 4.1 million foreign students in 2010 were enrolled in the developed nations that constitute the membership of OECD (2011, pp 358-63). From 2005 the rate of growth has been higher outside the OECD zone, including countries such as Malaysia and China, which have large numbers of cross-border students moving in both directions (OECD, 2010, pp 312-13, 334). The growth of mobility has not stopped there. Another large and increasing group of students is that engaged in study abroad for less than a year at a time (see, for example, IIE, 2011).

Figure 3.1 provides a summary of the global market in terms of national shares. As the figure shows, almost half of the world's foreign students, 48.9 per cent, are enrolled in the top five destination countries – the US, the UK, Australia, Germany and France. Between 2000 and 2010 the US's market share declined from 23 to 17 per cent and Germany's share dropped by two percentage points while the shares of the UK, Australia and New Zealand increased (OECD, 2011, p 363).

For the most part foreign students study in nations whose language has wide international recognition, not only the English-speaking nations, but France, Germany and Russia, and also China, where Putonghua may eventually become a second global language. The dominance (in absolute numbers) of English-speaking destinations reflects, among other factors, the progressive adoption of English as a global language. A growing number of institutions in the Nordic countries and the Netherlands especially, and in other parts of Western Europe and East Asia, now offer programmes in English 'to overcome their linguistic disadvantage in terms of attracting foreign students' (OECD, 2011, p 365). The main exceptions to this pattern of domination by world

Figure 3.1: Distribution of foreign tertiary students by nation of education (nation exporting educational services), 2010

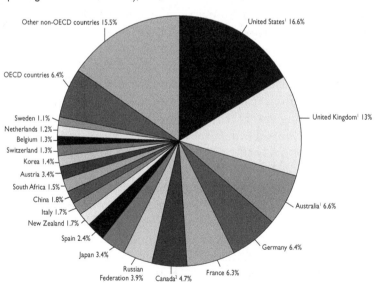

Notes: [1] Data relate to 'international', not 'foreign', students.

[2] Year of reference is 2009.

[3] Student numbers derived from varying sources, so caution should be used in interpretation.

Source: OECD (2011, p 364)

languages is Japan. In 2010 Japan attracted almost 3.4 per cent of the world total of international students, with more than 90 per cent of international students studying there coming from Asia (OECD, 2011, p 364). Students from China and Taiwan share a written language with Japan that gives them a start in learning Japanese as a spoken language.

Of the OECD countries, in 2010 the highest level of incoming student mobility, as measured by the ratio of international students to local tertiary students, was in Luxembourg, at 41 per cent, although this country is an outlier because of its high level of integration with neighbouring nations. Following Luxembourg were Australia (21.2 per cent), the UK (16 per cent), Austria and Switzerland (15.4 per cent each) and New Zealand (14.2 per cent). The UK, Australia and New Zealand have broadly similar commercial approaches to education export and parallel political regimes. The European nations within the list – Luxembourg, Austria and Switzerland – have mixed approaches but are more commercial for students coming from outside of Europe and less so for those coming from within. In the US international students were approximately 3.5 per cent of the total tertiary enrolment (OECD, 2011, pp 367-8).

In 2010 students coming from Asia constituted just over half, or 52.5 per cent, of the world's outgoing international students. Asian students represented 80 per cent of Australia's international students, 93 per cent of those studying in Japan and 95 per cent of those in Korea. Students from Asia were followed up in global significance by Europeans (22.7 per cent, the majority of them studying within Europe), Africans (11.8 per cent) and students from Latin America and the Caribbean (6.2 per cent). Students from mainland China were a colossal 19 per cent of all those enrolling in OECD nations, with another 1.2 per cent from Hong Kong, China. Their favourite destinations in order were the US (20 per cent), Australia (13.8 per cent) and Japan (13.6 per cent) (OECD, 2011, pp 369-70).

In terms of the structure of educational services, the majority of international education takes the form of programmes delivered in the country where the educational institution is headquartered, whereby the student crosses borders into the nation of education, that is, the form of international education discussed in this book. There are other forms, however. Some educational exporters set up branch campuses in the nation from which they draw their students. As noted in Chapter Two, this is called 'trans-national education' (McBurnie and Ziguras, 2006) and it is an especially important part of the education systems of Malaysia, Singapore, Hong Kong Special Administrative Region (SAR) and mainland China. Universities and colleges from the US,

Australia and the UK play a significant role in trans-national education in Asia. There are also trans-national institutions located in India, Latin America and several European countries. Branch campus provision is regulated by the receiving countries in which the learning takes place, and often also regulated for quality assurance in the country where the institution is headquartered. Other international mobility takes the form of electronic delivery of programmes, and other forms of distance education across borders.

Drivers of mobility and the political economy of education export

In its 2010 *Education at a glance* report, the OECD developed a detailed explanation for the growth of cross-border student mobility (OECD, 2010, pp 310-26). The drivers have changed over the years:

> The rise in the number of students enrolled abroad since 1975 stems from various factors. During the early years, public policies to promote and nurture academic, cultural, social and political ties between countries played a key role, especially in the context of the European construction: building mutual understanding among young Europeans was a major policy objective. North American policies of academic co-operation had similar rationales. Over time, however, economic factors played an increasing role. Decreasing transport costs, the spread of new technologies, and faster, cheaper communications made economies and societies increasingly interdependent during the 1980s and 1990s. The trend was particularly marked in the high-technology sector and in the labour market, as the internationalisation of labour markets for the highly skilled gave individuals an incentive to gain international experience as part of their studies. The spread of information and communication technologies (ICT) lowered the information and transaction costs of study abroad and boosted demand for international education. (OECD, 2010, p 313)

Growth in the internationalisation of tertiary education mirrors the globalisation of the wider economies and societies within which education takes place. As world economies converge at many points, and trade expands faster than production, there is a relative increase in demand for workers with intercultural skills, especially a facility in global English and knowledge of international business and common technologies. Individuals build their skill base through cross-border learning, and international education expands the potential for cross-country careers and migration to the country of education, or similar countries elsewhere. For their part, national economies gain from international student flows, in each direction, albeit for different reasons. When the nationals of one country train aboard, that builds cross-cultural capacity and international business potential. In some countries, where the demand for skilled professional labour, and the growth of education-hungry middle classes, are outstripping educational infrastructure, international education also supplements an inadequate educational supply at home. When other country nationals are educated at home, that helps to build a layer of professional workers who will be friendly to the country of education after they return. This has potential benefits for both the national economy and the foreign policy of the nation of education.

In some nations, those where full price tuition is charged, international education is an important source of surplus funding. It can also provide the nation of education with migrants who have a facility in global work, and occupationally specific skills. The free movement of workers within Europe encourages cross-border student mobility. Several OECD countries have eased their immigration policies to encourage international students to migrate. In 2010 Australia modified its policy to make migration of international student graduates more difficult, as discussed below, but it opened the doorway more broadly again in late 2011 (see also Chapter Five).

In recent years, in some English-speaking nations, international students have made a significant contribution to the size of the pool of skilled graduates available to the national economy. For the student, decisions about whether and where to go abroad are shaped by costs and benefits, hopes and expectations about future opportunity and trajectory, and factors of culture and identity including where they might feel comfortable and the professional direction they would like to take. The availability of information is another key element in decisions. Prospective students are influenced by the ratio between opportunities at home and opportunities abroad, by employment prospects as well as the education on offer, and affected by the reputations of nations, cities and individual educational institutions. Future migration potential is often a key driver, especially of passage into education in English-speaking nations and Western Europe. The availability of finance is a key element, and family members other than the student often share the costs of travel, tuition fees and living abroad, and help to shape the choices. In relation to the economics of student decision making about studying in other countries:

> For individuals, the returns from studying abroad depend largely on the policies of sending countries regarding financial aid to students going abroad and the tuition fee policies of countries of destination and the financial support they offer international students. The cost of living and exchange rates also affect the cost of international education. In addition, the long-term returns from international education depend greatly on how international degrees are recognised and valued by local labour markets. (OECD, 2010, p 311)

In most countries the tuition charges levied on individual international students are higher than those required of local students. However, only some countries see international education as a means of generating an economic surplus, charge tuition fees at commercial rates and encourage provider institutions to grow enrolments rapidly in the manner of a capitalist enterprise. This has become the norm in most of the English-speaking provider nations: the UK, Australia, New Zealand, Canada and Singapore. It also applies in parts of the non-profit sectors in the US, especially the community colleges, and in the North American for-profit sector as it does in for-profit institutions everywhere. Commercial international education is also the norm in the Malaysian private sector and in some institutions in Hong Kong, China and Western Europe.

A large group of countries charging higher fees to international students also partly subsidise them, often (but not always) while limiting the number of places for such students. In most European countries students from other European nations pay the same fees as home country students and lower tuition fees than students from outside the EU. EU students often enjoy arrangements similar to those that apply to local citizen students. Denmark is an extreme case of this kind of differential treatment. It charges no fees to students from home, EU countries and its partner Nordic countries Norway and Iceland, while students from non-EU countries pay full fees unless they are supported by Danish scholarships (OECD, 2010, pp 316-17, 2011, pp 365-7).

In Finland and Sweden neither local, EU nor non-EU foreign students pay fees. 'The fact that Finland, Iceland, Norway and Sweden do not have tuition fees for international students, combined with the existence of programmes taught in English, probably explains part of the robust growth in the number of foreign students enrolled in some of these countries between 2005 and 2010' (OECD, 2011, p 366). In Germany, in private institutions and those public institutions that charge fees, local and foreign students pay the same fees. Certain non-EU countries treat local and international students the same in formal terms: Norway, Iceland, Japan, Korea and the Russian Federation are included in this group. There are many scholarships for international students in Japan, from both government and private sources. In practice most international students in Korea also pay somewhat lower fees than local students. In both countries the number of foreign enrolments has grown sharply since 2000. In New Zealand international students in research degree programmes pay the same fees as local students, well below cost levels, a measure designed to strengthen research degree programmes that has been associated with the rapid growth of foreign research enrolments. In Australia all international students pay full fees aside from a small number who receive scholarships (OECD, 2010, pp 317-18). Australia and New Zealand have special partner country arrangements with each other that treat students as near-locals.

Doctoral education

The global doctoral market is shaped primarily not by tuition charges but by the availability and level of scholarship support. Doctoral students (and post-doctoral scholars) are especially prone to move, with about half of the mobile total moving into research universities in the US. Roughly half of the graduates from this group work in the US after graduation. Many become permanent migrants, including substantial numbers from developed nations such as the UK and Germany.

Advanced research programmes are much more internationalised than tertiary education as a whole. In 2010, international students accounted for more than 20 per cent of research degree enrolments in Australia (28.7 per cent), Austria (22.3 per cent), Belgium (18.5 per cent), Canada (20.5 per cent), New Zealand (37.2 per cent), Denmark (20.8 per cent), Switzerland (48.3 per cent, the highest in the OECD), the UK (41.7 per cent) and the US (27.8 per cent) (OECD, 2011, p 374).

Within the international student programme in Australia and New Zealand, however, research degree students are a relatively small part of the total of all international students – just 5 per cent in Australia and 7.6 per cent in New Zealand in 2010. International education in those countries is dominated by the more commercial, coursework component of the programme. International research degree study plays a much larger role in the US where 19.4 per cent of all international students entering US tertiary institutions, and closer to a third of those in the doctoral universities, are research degree students. The research degree share of international students is also high in Switzerland (25.4 per cent) and Sweden (15.3 per cent). In the UK the proportion is 8.9 per cent, pointing to the dual character of international education in that country, both commercial and research-focused; while in Japan the research student proportion is 9.9 per cent. In France research students constitute 11.5 per cent of foreign students (OECD, 2011, p 374). In all these nations scholarship policy is deployed to attract substantial cohorts of international talent. Doctoral students are primary contributors to the volume of research in developed innovation systems.

United States

There were 4,409 degree-granting institutions in the US in 2011, of which 1,676 were public with total revenues of US$267 billion, 1,629 not-for-profit private institutions ($69 billion) and 1,104 for-profit ($19 billion). The last was the fastest growing sector but enrolled just 9 per cent of all students in 2009. Only 270 US institutions were designated research universities, 165 in the public sector. In total 73 per cent of all higher education students were in the public sector and 33 per cent of the total were in community colleges. This gigantic and diverse system provides many options, but more than two thirds of all international students are concentrated in 200 US institutions (Green and Ferguson, 2011, pp 4-5).

Surveys of prospective students consistently find that the US is the most sought-after destination for international students. US higher education is the best resourced and highest in prestige, and the nation offers unparalleled career opportunities and a relatively open environment for high-skilled migrants. Nevertheless, international education is mostly not provided on an expansionary commercial basis. It is also relatively marginal in the life of higher education, aside from a small number of relatively internationalised institutions. International students constituted only 3.4 per cent of all enrolments in higher education in 2008, although because the US houses the second largest tertiary student population in the world after China, this proportion constitutes the largest single pool of cross-border students, and the industry contributed an estimated US$18.8 billion to the US economy in 2009-10 (Douglass et al, 2011). The major exception to the overall pattern of marginalisation of international education is at doctoral level. At this level international students constitute a large minority of total enrolments, and many research universities are dependent on graduate research assistants from China, India and other Asian nations, especially in engineering and technologies.

After the September 2001 attacks on the Pentagon and the World Trade Center in New York security regulation tightened and international student numbers in the 2003-06 period dropped, especially those from the Middle East and Southeast Asia, before returning to growth later in the decade. In 2001-02 international students were 3.7 per cent of all enrolled tertiary students. This level was the historic highpoint, and despite increasing rates of growth, the system still had not returned to it in 2009-10 (IIE, 2011). Figure 3.2 shows the long-term historic trend.

Figure 3.2: Number and proportion of international students in US higher education 1949-50 to 2009-10, five-year intervals

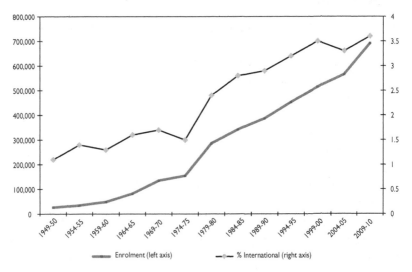

Source: IIE (2011)

Between 2000 and 2008 the share of the world's foreign students located in the US dropped from 26 to 18 per cent (OECD, 2010, p 314). The US housed the largest number of students from China and India, as well as 61.5 per cent of all international students moving out of Korea in 2008. The number of students from China rose sharply from 98,235 in 2008-09 to 127,628 in 2009-10, an increase of 29.9 per cent. If not for this substantial increase overall international student numbers would have fallen in 2009-10. Table 3.1 lists the top 10 student source countries in 2008-09 and 2009-10.

A feature of Table 3.1 is the variation in level of study by national origin. The majority of students from India, Taiwan China, Turkey and mainland China were enrolled in US tertiary education at graduate level. Most of the students from Vietnam, Japan, Korea, Mexico and Saudi Arabia were enrolled at lower levels.

Table 3.1: Nations of origin of international students in US higher education in 2008-09 and 2009-10, top 10 nations

Nation of student origin (importing nation)	Students 2008-09	Students 2009-10	Change in numbers	Proportion of international students in 2009-10	Proportion of these students at graduate level, 2009-10
			%	%	%
China, mainland	98,235	127,628	29.9	18.5	52.1
India	103,260	104,897	1.6	15.2	65.1
Korea	75,065	72,153	–3.9	10.4	32.4
Canada	29,697	28,145	–5.2	4.1	42.5
Taiwan China	28,065	26,685	–4.9	3.9	54.8
Japan	29,264	24,842	–15.1	3.6	21.7
Saudi Arabia	12,661	15,810	24.9	2.3	22.0
Mexico	14,850	13,450	–9.4	1.9	29.1
Vietnam	12,823	13,112	2.2	1.9	18.7
Turkey	12,148	12,397	2.0	1.8	53.1
All nations	671,616	690,923	2.9	100.0	42.3

Source: IIE (2011)

International students were distributed unevenly among US higher education institutions. More than one quarter of the total was enrolled in California (13.9 per cent of US international students) and New York. A small number of US doctoral universities had sizeable international populations at first-degree level. In 2009–10 the largest number of international students at all levels was at the University of Southern California (USC) in Los Angeles, with 7,987 students. USC's motivation was not financial – the international students paid the same tuition fees as USC's domestic students. Rather, the high international student intake helped create a 'more global university' and boosted USC's standing in national rankings because the international students achieved substantially higher test scores than the domestic students (Douglass et al, 2011). Table 3.2 lists the 20 largest international student cohorts in US higher education institutions in 2009-10.

Table 3.2: Largest international student enrolments in US universities, 2009-10

Institution	Number of international students	Proportion of total student enrolment
		%
University of Southern California	7,987	22.9
University of Illinois, Urbana-Champaign	7,287	16.7
New York University	7,276	16.8
Purdue University, main campus	6,903	16.8
Columbia University	6,833	28.2
University of Michigan, Ann Arbor	6,095	14.6
University of California, Los Angeles	6,585	14.3
Michigan State University	5,358	11.3
University of Texas, Austin	5,265	10.3
Boston University	5,172	16.4
University of Florida	4,920	9.7
State University of New York, Buffalo	4,911	17.0
Harvard University	4,867	18.4
Indiana University, Bloomington	4,819	11.4
Ohio State University, main campus	4,796	8.7
University of Minnesota, Twin Cities	4,665	9.0
Texas A&M University	4,611	9.4
Penn State University, University Park	4,561	10.3
University of Pennsylvania	4,522	18.5
Arizona State University	4,483	6.6

Source: IIE (2011)

As noted, the role of international students was more significant at doctoral stage. In the ten campuses of the University of California (UC) system, in 2009-10, 18 per cent of graduate students were foreign nationals, including 27 per cent at Berkeley. This compared with just 4 per cent of UC first degree enrolments.

However, 'there is a new goal at the UC-wide level to raise the number of out-of-state US and international students to 10 per cent, largely to draw increased income' (Douglass et al, 2011). There were substantial reductions in government funding of many US public universities in the wake of the global financial crisis, which began in late 2008 (although its roots date back further) and led to sharp falls in state government taxation revenues. The cuts continued into the next decade. For example, in 2011-12 29 state governments planned reductions in their higher education budgets, including US$1.5 billion in California. Not surprisingly, as stated in a 2011 report on US higher education commissioned by Australian Education International, 'recruitment of international students is receiving greater attention as a revenue source' (quoted in Green and Ferguson, 2011, pp 2, 15-17). Some institutions decided to recruit international students more vigorously in order to generate revenues. For example, Ohio State University decided to increase its international student enrolment from 3,600 to 5,400. Colorado State University opened a recruiting office in Shanghai with three part-time staff. The Regents of the University of California decided to pursue increased international and out-of-state enrolment to compensate for lost state funding (Green and Ferguson, 2011, p 16). The growing emphasis on recruitment coincided with increased activity by US universities offshore, such as New York University's decision to open a branch campus in Shanghai. State international trade officers began to assist some institutions (Green and Ferguson, 2011, p 17).

Nevertheless, most doctoral universities in the US have yet to adopt the fully commercial approach used in the UK, Australia and New Zealand. There is a widespread perception that international students take places that might otherwise be provided to local students, particularly in the public institutions. Places in the most prestigious institutions that tend to draw international student demand are very scarce. Moreover, many US institutions have only one international recruiter, and few use international education agents in the manner of institutions in the UK and Australia, which recruit large populations via that medium even though agents play a central role in international education in some countries, notably China. Some US institutions are prevented from paying commission to recruiting agents who provide international students, by state spending rules (Green and Ferguson, 2011, p 18).

Canada

Canada is a significant competitor for Australia and New Zealand, particularly in relation to students from China and Korea, although little challenge to their market share in Southeast Asia. Canadian universities are of relatively high quality and sound reputation, Canada offers relatively safe and well-serviced urban settings, and it also offers prospective students a potential stepping-stone to the nearby US. In the 2000s some Canadian institutions adopted more vigorous recruitment with the intention of using full fee international education as a revenue source. The Canadian government expanded its promotion of the export sector, creating a new 'education brand' for Canada and using trade commissioners to promote education in key export zones. 'The Department of Foreign Affairs and International Trade Canada highlighted the importance of international education as a key export in a 2008 report measuring the economic value of international students in Canada. It was found that the international students added US$6.5 billion to the Canadian economy, and employed up to 83,000 Canadians in 2008' (Deloitte Access Economics, 2011, pp 47–8).

Unlike the UK and Australia in the 2009-11 period, Canada did not introduce new restrictions on permanent migration and student visas. Instead it refined its Skilled Migration Program to facilitate students who wanted to stay in Canada to work after graduation. This may assist Canada to expand international education numbers at the expense of the UK and Australia.

United Kingdom

The UK is the world's second largest destination for cross-border students, and houses the higher education system that in international education is most similar to, and competitive with, those of Australia and New Zealand. The UK was the first nation to introduce full fee commercial international education as a means of generating revenues to fund tertiary education. However, as in Australia, after strong growth in international education in the mid-2000s, the UK introduced a more restrictive approach to student visas and the migration of international student graduates.

In 2008-09 there were 368,970 international students in higher education in the UK, of whom 304,785 were in England and 37,545 in Scotland. Of these students 117,660 were from EU member countries and 251,310 from outside the EU. The total number of students had increased by 13.2 per cent since 2007-08. Altogether 15 per cent of all higher education students were international, but the proportion was much higher in taught postgraduate degrees (43 per cent) and research postgraduate degrees (43 per cent, and 50 per cent of full-time students). As in the US and Australia, in the UK the two largest source countries were the demographic powerhouses China and India. While numbers from China increased slightly in 2008-09 there was a sharp growth in numbers from India – the reverse of the pattern in the US (UKCISA, 2011). Australia and the UK recruited similar numbers of students from both China and India. (In relation to India, the trajectory of the two exporters diverged somewhat in 2009-10. Following reputational damage to Australian education in India, the flow of Indian students into Australia dropped sharply; this did not happen in the UK.) Australia was the stronger exporter in Southeast Asia, especially Indonesia, but both nations took in significant cohorts from Malaysia.

Table 3.3 lists the top 10 source countries for international students in the UK, five of which were in the EU and five of which were not and entailed full-cost fees.

Table 3.3: Nations of origin of international students in UK higher education in 2007-08 and 2008-09, top 10 nations

Nation of student origin (importing nation)	Students 2007-08	Students 2008-09	Change in numbers	Proportion of international students in 2008-09
			%	%
China	45,355	47,035	3.7	12.7
India	25,905	34,065	31.5	9.2
Republic of Ireland (EU)	15,260	15,360	0.7	4.2
United States	13,905	14,345	3.2	3.9
Nigeria	11,785	14,380	22.0	3.9
Germany (EU)	13,625	14,130	3.7	3.8
France (EU)	12,685	13,090	3.2	3.6
Malaysia	11,730	12,695	11.7	3.4
Greece (EU)	12,625	12,035	−4.7	3.3
Cyprus (EU)	9640	10,370	7.6	2.8
All nations	325,985	368,970	13.2	100.0

Source: UKCISA (2011)

Of the EU international students in 2008-09, 12,555 (10.7 per cent) were postgraduate research students, while of the non-EU students 27,720 (11.0 per cent) were in that category. As in the US, international enrolments were concentrated in certain leading research universities. The cohorts of non-EU students in 2008-09 were slightly larger than the cohorts of international students in the US, but not as large in absolute terms as in Australian institutions (Chapter Five), although large in proportional terms, led by 68 per cent at the London School of Economics and Political Science (LSE). The largest absolute enrolment of non-EU students was 8,800 at the University of Manchester. Table 3.4 has details.

In 2010 non-EU students paid an average of £10,463 per year for Arts and £11,435 for Science, although tuition fees in some programmes were higher, such as £26,250 in lab-based courses at Imperial College London (Partridge, 2010, p 37).

In all there were another 388,135 students studying wholly overseas for a UK higher education qualification in 2008-09. Of these 190,865 were registered at a UK higher education institution – 9,885 at an overseas campus, 112,385 in some form of distance programme and

Table 3.4: Largest non-EU international student enrolments in UK universities, 2008-09

Institution	Number of non-EU international students	Proportion of total student enrolment
		%
University of Manchester	8,800	23
University of Nottingham	7,900	24
University College London	7,125	34
University of Warwick	7,080	25
LSE	6,555	68
University of Oxford	6,020	25
London Metropolitan University	5,810	22
University of the Arts, London	5,750	20
University of Leeds	5,690	18
University of Northumbria, Newcastle	5,650	17
University of Greenwich	5,555	21
University of Birmingham	5,550	19
University of Edinburgh	5,485	22
University of Cambridge	5,430	24
University of Westminster	5,420	23
Imperial College of STM	5,385	38
City University	5,345	25
University of Sheffield	5,295	21
University of Bedfordshire	5,165	30
King's College London	4,875	22

Notes: LSE = London School of Economics and Political Science; Imperial College of STM = Imperial College and Science, Technology and Medicine.

Source: UKCISA (2011)

68,595 involved in joint degrees and other forms of collaborative provision. A further 197,275 were studying for a UK award through a partner institution or similar arrangement (UKCISA, 2011). In addition, another group of international students were enrolled in UK further education. In 2006-07 there were 84,340 such students, including 37,955 non-EU students, of whom 35,005 were in institutions in England. Much the largest national source of international students for UK further education was Poland (16,455) followed by India (4,735), Ireland (4,580) and mainland China (3,985) (UKCISA, 2011).

According to the OECD, non-EU international students brought £2.2 billion to the UK in tuition revenues as well as generating other revenues and economic activity (Partridge, 2010, p 37). However, after the election of the UK Coalition government in 2010 immigration policy began to shift. In September 2010 the UK Immigration Minister noted that only about half of the recent student visas had been for degree-level study, with many students entering UK private vocational colleges and language schools. 'The Minister cast doubt on whether these students were benefiting themselves or Britain, alluding to the impact of unscrupulous agents in India, and suggesting that changes would be made to the immigration system to make it more difficult for students to remain in the UK after completing their studies' (Deloitte Access Economics, 2011, p 45). The resulting UK policy changes closely paralleled the changes to official policy and regulation in Australia (see Chapter Five), except that in the UK permanent migration was reduced by more than in Australia (Deloitte Access Economics, 2011, p 46), and there was no reversal of the restrictive policy as was to happen in Australia in late 2011.

In March 2011 a new UK visa regime for students was announced. This entailed a higher required level of English language proficiency; no accompaniment by student dependants except for postgraduate university students and government-sponsored students; restrictions of most students to no more than five years of study; and withdrawal of the previous right of graduates to seek two years of employment after graduation unless certain kinds of skilled job were available. According to the British Home Secretary, 'the old student visa regime failed to control immigration and failed to protect legitimate students from poor quality colleges' (Jobbins, 2011). The UK government still hoped to attract significant numbers of full fee students, but aimed to largely decouple educational participation from migration.

Countering the downward pressure on enrolments were the changes to funding arrangements in UK higher education, beginning in 2012, which was expected to lead to a reduction in non-research funding from £7.1 to £4.2 billion in 2014-15. 'With fees for English students to be capped at £9,000 per year, foreign students will continue to represent an attractive revenue stream' (Partridge, 2010, p 37). As in Australia the desire of institutions to increase enrolments for economic reasons, and the official strategy of using international education to build the national skill base, conflicted directly with the government's restrictive visa regime.

Asia-Pacific region

The Asia-Pacific region has seen a continuous increase in both the import and export of educational services, with some nations – Japan, China, Malaysia and Singapore – playing a significant role in student movement in both directions.

Japan has had a highly developed higher education system for nearly half a century, enabling it to become an important exporter. In 2010 Japan's target for international student numbers was revised upwards to 300,000. After 1990 it became clear that research universities in Hong Kong SAR, Taiwan, Korea and Singapore were on track to achieve Western European levels of performance, and after 2000 it became increasingly apparent that higher education in China was on course to become the second major national system in the world, after that of the US. In the late 2000s Malaysia planned to reach a target of 100,000 international students by 2020, while Singapore's target was a more ambitious 150,000 students by 2015. China has set itself a target of 500,000 international students by 2020 (Goddard, 2011). India has only a minor role in export.

There is growing student mobility within the region, particularly between the nations of East Asia, which are principal zones of export and import for each other. Formal recognition protocols and student exchange schemes emerged more slowly than private student movement but are expected to facilitate further growth in mobility in the decade of the 2010s. Given the overall expansion of the East Asian middle classes and the continued demand for English language immersion it is unlikely that in itself intra-Asian educational mobility – and more generally, the role of educational export in Asian nations – will undermine the global market position of higher education in Australia and New Zealand, all else being equal. The size of the expected incremental increase in the middle class in China alone dwarfs not just the size of higher education in Australia and New Zealand, but also the whole populations of those countries. In this context there is plenty of room for all-round growth in education exports.

Nevertheless, Asian destinations pose a competitive challenge as magnets for high quality students, including doctoral students. Singapore has established a role as a global educational 'hub' and Hong Kong seeks to do likewise. Malaysia has the same aspiration: its research universities are not strong enough in capacity or reputation to achieve a parallel function to that of Singapore, but it has been able to draw a sizeable cohort of students from the Islamic world, with more students from Arab nations than Australia (see Table 3.5). Japan's research sector and aid-based scholarships draw many Asian students, and China's universities, where research is growing rapidly, will do so increasingly in future. The elite Chinese universities in the 985 group, including Peking and Tsinghua, are more internationalised in their outlooks, their staff and student composition and their activities, than is the case in the second and third tier institutions.

Table 3.5: Tertiary education export in the East Asia-Pacific region, selected countries, 2009

Nation of education (exporting nation)	Number of students entering that nation from:				
	East Asia and Pacific	South and West Asia	Arab states	Other including Europe and Africa	Total
Australia	154,662	42,140	7284	53,551	257,637
New Zealand	19,537	6435	699	11,680	38,351
UK	93,961	54,572	20,383	200,052	368,968
USA	284,129	127,771	26,621	222,060	660,581
Canada[1]	30,647	8353	7192	46,689	92,881
China	na	na	na	na	61,211
Hong Kong SAR	8,906	50	0	289	9245
Macau SAR	14,171	6	0	181	14,358
Japan	116,066	4,872	713	9,948	131,599
Korea	43,267	1,436	165	5,162	50,030
Indonesia	2,891	11	17	104	3,023
Malaysia	16,395	9,362	7,561	7,992	41,310
Singapore	na	na	na	na	40,401
Thailand	12,794	1,242	49	2,276	16,361
Vietnam	na	na	na	na	4,207
Philippines	1,559	438	35	633	2,665
Fiji	7,282	14	na	na	7,444

Notes: 1 Public institutions only. na = not available.

Source: UNESCO (2011)

In China domestic provision is expanding rapidly, suggesting an enhanced capacity to enrol international students. There were 31 million higher education students in 2010, an increase of 35 per cent since 2005. As noted, China's official target is 500,000 international students by 2020 and to achieve this target it is cooperating with the EU, the Association of Southeast Asian Nations (ASEAN) and regional blocs in Africa, the Arab World and Latin America. By 2011 mutual degree recognition agreements had been signed with 34 countries. China provides a relatively generous scholarship programme for African students, which is part of a broader strategy of investment in the African Continent (Murray, 2011, pp 20-1).

Conclusion

In describing and assessing the global market for cross-border education, some trends appear to be contradictory. National motivations for internationalisation tend to vary. The drive for revenues and the desire for global market share are not identical across the world – more governments are focused on market share than on revenues per se, and by no means are all governments concerned about market share. Nation-states that pursue highly commercialised strategies involving mainly full-fee enrolments can and do also pursue some policies – such as the tightening of migration through education – which work against the primary objective of the market strategy. The UK and Australia are prominent recent examples. Among individual institutions, educational reputation and quality are not predictive of either motivations for internationalisation or the extent of actually achieved internationalisation.

The one trend that is clear is continued growth in the global market. This, in turn, is associated with a fairly stable hierarchy of export nations, although Australia and more recently New Zealand have risen within this hierarchy. All in all, the global roles of Australia and New Zealand are remarkable, given the size of the two populations. This is discussed further in the next chapter.

FOUR

'There's gold in them thar students!' Australia and New Zealand in the global market

Introduction

In the period between 2000 and 2010, among the developed nations of the OECD, Australia and New Zealand (and particularly the latter) increased their global market share sharply. Inward student mobility into these two European heritage nations on the border of Asia increased more rapidly than in other OECD nations. This was not only because of a relatively favourable location next to the fast moving zones of economic development in East and Southeast Asia. For most of the 1990s and 2000s the Australian and New Zealand governments encouraged the rapid growth of international education as a source of revenue and of human capital via the inward migration of graduates, although Australia took a different approach in 2009-11 (as did the UK at the same time). Growth was continuous in Australia until 2010, and while, as discussed later in Chapter Six, there were fluctuations in New Zealand, as enrolments from East Asia rose and fell, the longer-term pattern has been one of significant growth. On their side, education institutions in Australia and New Zealand have had strong economic incentives to increase international student numbers. Formal regulation has mostly encouraged the export sectors to drive their own activity and growth. The characteristics and the significance of this are central themes within the remaining chapters of this book.

This chapter provides an overview discussion of the evolution of market share in Australia and New Zealand. It also discusses the problems and prospects of cross-border education in the two countries as at the time of writing. The chapter provides the political economy backdrop for the detailed discussion of regulation in the two nations that follows in Chapters Five and Six.

Export sector in Australia

Prior to the 1985 Australian legislation that established the international education market, the main focus of international education was aid-based and designed to assist the processes of modernisation and development in Asian nations. The underlying strategic objective of the Colombo Plan, launched in 1951, was to steer post-colonial nations in Asia away from communism by shaping the outlook of their future leaders. But there were also unplanned effects in Australia itself. The Colombo Plan students participated in Australian higher education at a time when the White Australia policy was still in force and played a crucial part in breaking it down. The Colombo Plan pioneered a different education system in a different Australia. Not only was there a significant number of these scholarship students, over time the number of private international students in subsidised places subject to quota also grew, and eventually the private students outnumbered the scholarship students. This second group suggested the potential for commercial marketing. But it was only after the UK government established a category of full fee-paying students that Australia took this initiative.

The federal government's Jackson committee first proposed the commercial approach in 1984. Once implemented, the government followed through with force. The commercial market was made the organising framework for all international education in tertiary institutions. From 1990 all subsidised places for private students, the last vestige of the pre-market era, were abolished. The only exceptions to the commercial framework were a small number of scholarship places maintained for foreign aid purposes. Student numbers and fee levels were fully deregulated, enabling universities to run international education as an expansionary capitalist business largely distinct in the financial sense from the provision of educational services for local students. The federal government coordinated the early recruitment of fee-paying students. In 1990 Australian education centres were created in nine countries, managed in conjunction with diplomatic missions. In 1994 educational counsellors were added to Australian diplomatic posts. Later, in 1997, Australian Education International was formed and integrated with the federal Department of Education, responsible for both the promotion and regulation of the industry. The first Education Services for Overseas Students (ESOS) Act, providing for consumer protection, was passed in 1991.

Thus the revenue-raising objective became dominant in international education. The secondary policy objectives were to engage with Asia and build a pro-Australian constituency in the importing nations. Later, in the first half of the 2000s, the international education programme was also used to augment skilled migration, and international students became a major source of new citizens.

In 2009 there were 185 institutions in Australia with government approval to offer higher education courses, including 37 public and seven self-accrediting private institutions. The latter included two foreign universities with small enrolments, Carnegie-Mellon and Heriot-Watt. There were 141 non self-accrediting institutions, including 105 faith-based or private entities. The private sector accounted for approximately 10 per cent of all international enrolments. In the specialist English language colleges three quarters of enrolments were in the private sector (Murray, 2011, pp 3-4). From 1987 onwards the number of fee-paying students expanded more quickly than expected. Figure 4.1 illustrates the growth in international education enrolments between 1994 and 2011, also showing the trend in higher education enrolments. (Note that there is a series break between 2001 and 2002, with a change in the method of data collection, and that some students enrolled in more than one sector of education in the same year.)

In 2010 total international education enrolments fell for the first time, mostly because of a sharp fall in enrolments in the English language colleges. Table 4.1 shows the trend in enrolments by sector of education, between 2005 and 2010. As in New Zealand, the nations of origin were unevenly spread across the different sectors of education. Students from Korea, and to a lesser extent Japan and Brazil, were especially strongly represented in English language colleges. Students from India and Nepal were over-represented in vocational education and training (VET) and responsible for much of its growth. Students from China, Hong Kong SAR, Malaysia and Singapore were mostly located in higher education institutions.

The fortunes of Australia's international education industry are unequivocally tied to Asia, especially Southeast and East Asia. Among the English language countries Australia is the largest exporter of tertiary education to Malaysia and Indonesia and the second largest exporter, after the US, in relation to Vietnam. In relation to students from China, Australia is the third exporter after the US and Japan (OECD, 2010, 2011).

Data on student numbers collected by the federal education department in Australia reveals that, for higher education only, in 2009 all but two of the top 15 sources for international students were located in Asia. Table 4.2 provides details. The largest source populations were from China (much the most important), Singapore, Malaysia, India and

Hong Kong SAR. Between 2008 and 2009 numbers from Vietnam and Saudi Arabia increased rapidly, while those from the US and Hong Kong fell. The drop in enrolments of US students may have been due to the effects of the global financial crisis in that country. (Note that these data include offshore enrolments. In total, 245,593 of all international students were enrolled onshore in Australia, 76.5 per cent of the total.)

Figure 4.1: International student enrolments, Australia, all sectors of education and higher education, 1994-2011

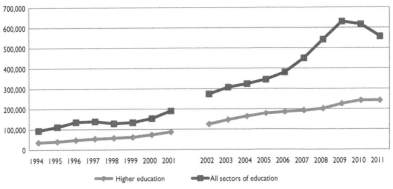

Source: AEI (2012)

Table 4.1: International education enrolments by education sector, Australia, 2005-10

Education sector	2005	2006	2007	2008	2009	2010
Higher education	177,864	185,449	192,223	202,270	226,011	243,591
VET	50,919	67,018	101,988	153,881	207,985	206,581
Schooling	25,096	24,479	26,765	28,303	27,380	24,235
ELICOs	64,560	76,905	102,214	127,247	137,539	113,477
Other	26,257	26,437	27,331	30,122	31,748	31,235
Total	344,696	380,288	450,521	541,823	630,663	619,119

Notes: VET = vocational education and training; ELICOs = English language colleges.

Source: AEI (2011)

Unlike New Zealand, Australia has only a small role in educating students born in the Pacific, aside for the student children of parents who have migrated permanently to Australia. Efforts to develop South America as a major market have largely been unsuccessful. Some individual Australian institutions have developed healthy flows of students from European nations such as Norway and Germany, but Europe is not a major source region overall. Like New Zealand, Australian higher education attracts a solid cohort of students from the US each year, and a smaller group from Canada.

Table 4.2: Nations of origin of international students in higher education, Australia, 2008 and 2009, top 15 nations

Nation of student origin (importing nation)	Students in 2008	Students in 2009	Change between 2008 and 2009	Proportion of international students in 2009
			%	%
China (mainland)	65,159	78,181	20.0	24.4
Singapore	32,174	33,485	4.1	10.4
Malaysia	31,227	33,218	6.4	10.4
India	27,339	27,837	1.8	8.7
Hong Kong SAR	22,275	21,147	−5.1	6.5
Vietnam	10,038	13,117	30.7	4.1
Indonesia	11,703	12,040	2.9	3.8
United States	9,856	8,305	−15.7	2.6
Korea	6,415	6,909	7.7	2.2
Sri Lanka	5,072	5,362	5.7	1.7
Canada	4,843	4,930	1.8	1.5
Thailand	4,663	4,649	−0.3	1.4
United Arab Emirates	3,968	4,153	4.7	1.3
Nepal	3,269	3,865	18.2	1.2
Saudi Arabia	2,028	3,785	86.6	1.2
Total	294,163	320,970	9.1	100.0

Notes: 'Nation of student origin' refers to country of permanent residence.

Source: DEEWR (2011)

A relatively high proportion of international students in Australian higher education were enrolled in Business Studies programmes in 2009: 167,161 in total, 52.1 per cent of all international students, including 51,541 students in taught Master's programmes. A total of 27,115 students were in Information Technology and 24,787 in Engineering and related technologies, with 22,728 in Health Sciences. Just 11,996 students (3.7 per cent) were enrolled in doctoral programmes, with the largest cohorts in Natural and Physical Sciences, Engineering, and Humanities and Social Science programmes (DEEWR, 2011).

In 2009 10 Australian institutions had more than 8,000 international students onshore in Australia, meaning their international student populations were larger than the USC, the institution with the biggest international enrolment in the US in 2009-10. A further eight institutions had more than 6,000 international students onshore. When offshore enrolments were included, 13 Australian institutions had more than 8,000 international students and five had more than 12,000 students.

The largest onshore enrolment was the 13,052 at Monash University in Melbourne, and the largest total international enrolment 24,710 at RMIT University in the same city. Table 4.3 lists the 18 institutions with the largest onshore enrolment.

Table 4.3: International student enrolments in Australian higher education, 2009: 18 universities with the largest onshore enrolment

Institution	Onshore international students	Onshore international students as a proportion of onshore students	Total international students	International student fees as a proportion of university income
		%		%
Monash University	13,052	25.2	21,114	18.8
University of Melbourne	11,995	26.4	12,005	17.9
University of Sydney	11,928	23.7	11,969	17.4
Macquarie University	11,455	33.4	12,402	30.4
University of New South Wales	11,433	24.7	11,487	17.2
Griffith University	10,115	25.8	10,886	20.1
Curtin University of Technology	9,667	27.7	8,476	21.6
RMIT University	9,460	27.8	24,710	28.0
University of Queensland	8,826	21.7	8,826	14.9
University of Technology, Sydney	8,238	24.4	8,273	22.0
Central Queensland University	7,682	40.1	7,736	35.8
Swinburne University of Technology	7,025	35.9	9,518	25.3
Deakin University	7,024	19.4	7,652	19.4
University of Southern Queensland	7,005	27.9	7,005	16.9
University of Ballarat	6,568	56.6	7,851	28.9
Queensland University of Technology	6,302	15.6	6,403	13.4
La Trobe University	6,222	21.2	7,501	16.3
University of South Australia	6,148	21.1	13,426	19.0
All public universities	245,593	25.0	320,970	na

Note: na = data not available.

Source: DEEWR (2011)

Economic impact of the industry

As the final column of Table 4.3 shows, in 2009 international student fees were a major component of institutional revenues in higher education in Australia. In that year they constituted more than 20 per cent of income in eight universities, led by 35.8 per cent at Central Queensland University and 30.4 per cent at Macquarie University (DEEWR, 2011). In 2010 revenues from fees and charges were expected to total an average of 18 per cent of the income of all higher education institutions on the public register (Deloitte Access Economics, 2011, p vi). According to the Australian Bureau of Statistics, international education generated a total of AUD$7.018 billion in tuition fees in 2009-10, including $3.768 billion in higher education institutions and $2.033 billion in vocational education in current prices (ABS, 2011).

Between 1998-99 and 2009-10 the total volume of education exports rose from AUD$3.391 billion to $18.507 billion in current prices. Higher education exports totalled $10.632 billion, vocational education $5.134 billion. This includes both international student fees and other spending by the students and their families. Education jumped from 12.1 to 35.1 per cent of all services exports (ABS, 2011). As Australian trade debits for education are low, typically 5 per cent or less of the value of trade credits, nearly all of this total of $18.5 billion in export revenue is returned to the national economy as net benefit on the trade account.

Australian Bureau of Statistics data suggest average spending per international student in higher education was AUD$55,205 in 2009, including an average $19,837 in tuition fees and $35,368 in living costs. The corresponding figures for VET were $10,360 in fees and $16,453 in living costs, totalling $26,813. Spending by all students was $10.821 billion in higher education, $5.068 billion in vocational education, $1.090 billion in English language colleges and $0.945 billion in schools. Together with spending by students in 'other' institutions of $0.612 billion this totalled $18.535 billion (Deloitte Access Economics, 2011, p 4). Table 4.4 shows how the export income was distributed through the economy.

Deloitte Access Economics estimated that in 2009, international education generated the equivalent of 180,805 full-time jobs, with 127,653 generated directly and 53,153 indirectly. Of these jobs 104,705 resulted from international students in higher education, 73,302 directly (Deloitte Access Economics, 2011, p 6). In the 2008-11 period education ranked as Australia's third or fourth largest export sector, behind coal and iron ore, and duelling with gold for third position. The position of gold fluctuated with the commodity price.

Table 4.4: International student spending as distributed through the economy, Australia, 2009

Industry sector	International student spending	Proportion of total international student spending
	AUD$ million	%
Education	7,090	0.38
Other property services	3,028	0.16
Retail trade	3,010	0.16
Air transport	2,125	0.11
Accommodation, restaurants	1,911	0.10
Communications	336	0.02
Road transport	335	0.02
Rail and other transport	226	0.01
Banking and insurance	164	0.01
Movies, radio and television	124	0.01
Libraries, museums, arts	124	0.01
Other	62	<0.01
Total	18,535	1.00

Source: Deloitte Access Economics (2011, p 5)

Change in migration policy

For most of the 2000s the nexus between international education and migration was strong. Each year between 2001 and 2005 approximately 50,000 student visas were converted to permanent residencies. About one third of international students became permanent residents. Net overseas migration peaked at almost 300,000 per annum in 2008-09, much of it due to international student visas – which were included in the calculation of net overseas migration – and the subsequent throughput into permanent resident status (Goddard, 2011). Graduates accessed migration through a points-based system that discriminated between different fields of study on the basis of national economic need. A frankly migration-oriented education industry evolved, centred on business partnerships between education agents in South Asia focused on the provision of migration routes via tertiary education, and private colleges in Australia. International students were recruited in large numbers into the fields of occupational training listed as 'preferred' for migration purposes. Graduates from those programmes enjoyed an advantage in applications for permanent residence. Training programmes in occupations such as accounting, hairdressing and cooking underwent a boom in enrolments. Total enrolments in vocational education and training grew especially rapidly from 2005 (50,919) to 2009 (207,985). 'By 2008-09, former temporary migrants represented more than a third of the entire permanent migration program' (Deloitte Access Economics, 2011, p 34).

From late 2008 onwards it became apparent that the politics of migration was changing. In the wake of the global financial crisis there were cuts to the skilled labour migration intake in late 2008 and early 2009. Polls suggested that public opinion was becoming more unfavourable to migration, even as a series of violent attacks on students from South Asia were reported in the media in Australia and India (Deloitte Access Economics, 2011, p 35). There was also growing criticism of the employability of international student graduates, particularly those from vocational training. The criticisms focused on both the English language skills of graduates and on the suitability of their training programmes for workforce needs. There were also allegations that some colleges provided sham training programmes and operated as nothing but clearing houses for migration.

In the 2010 election both sides of politics stated a commitment to reductions in net migration. Even before the election the Labor Party government began to change the migration policy settings so as to reduce net overseas migration to about half the earlier level. These changes bore down heavily on international education at both the point of entry of students and the passage from graduate status to permanent migration. (Only those aspects of the policy changes that affected market supply will be discussed here. Further considerations are addressed in Chapter Five.) The federal government moved to tighten the regulation of institutions that provided international education. Some private colleges that were found to have provided sham or substandard training programmes, or mishandled student fees after closures to particular programmes, were closed. At the same time, the requirements for student visas became more difficult to fulfil.

Prospective students from China, Vietnam and India had to be able to demonstrate that they had enough financial support in advance to cover the full period of study, which could be several years. The required annual rate of support was raised from AUD$12,000 to $18,000 per year. A family whose student child planned four years of study had to demonstrate a bank deposit of at least $72,000 for a period of six months or more – a condition not even many affluent business families could fulfil, as money is rarely left idle for that length of time. These financial requirements were much tougher than those applied in the US. Visa processing was also slowed, with delays of three months or more becoming the norm. Again this was slower than in competitor countries. Migration regulation was also altered. The requirements for permanent residence status were steepened. Graduates had to pass an English language test and/or meet the expectation of a period of work in the occupation in which they had trained, a difficult condition to fulfil. The preferred occupations list was abolished. After a hiatus during which there was no list of preferred occupations, the subsequent new points system shifted the emphasis to a small number of high skill occupations, and awarded additional points not just to Australian but internationally gained qualifications. 'Overall, in terms of gaining points for a graduate Skilled Migration application, there is little incentive to gain an Australian qualification over a recognised overseas qualification' (Deloitte Access Economics, 2011, p 33).

These changes made it more difficult to migrate. In addition, a rising Australian dollar made a sojourn in that country less economically attractive, having a profound impact in the market. Demand for Australian education in India and Nepal fell sharply. In India the effects of the crackdown on private training colleges, and the agents supporting them, compounded in an especially virulent manner with media-fed controversy about the violence affecting South Asian students in Australia. However, it should be emphasised that the main overall trigger of change in the industry, especially outside the sub-continent, were policy-driven reductions in educational supply. In an industry in which the providers still needed revenues, supply shapes demand much more than vice versa. In this case the reduction in supply triggered automatic reductions in demand in all of the source countries, as education agents and families switched their attention from Australia to alternative destinations such as the US and Canada. The downward trend in applications for student visas, visas granted, and the flow of students into Australia, spread from the Indian subcontinent to China, Vietnam and Southeast Asia in general.

The policy changes were designed to weaken the nexus between migration and education, and thereby slow the flow of incoming students without directly interfering with market forces in arbitrary fashion, while also shoring up the reputation of Australian institutions abroad and reworking the contribution of international education to the pool of human capital. These objectives were not altogether congruent. A major change in the regulation of both education and migration that rendered Australia less welcoming of international students, triggering both a sharp reduction in supply and a dramatic shift in demand, was likely to have negative consequences for the national education brand and for the export revenue flows the brand helped to sustain. So it proved to be.

Many students halfway through their programmes in the 2009-10 period lost the expected opportunity to migrate. These changes fed back to the student source countries, reinforcing the message that Australia had become less welcoming to international students. There is little doubt that the federal government intended this, despite the cost to export revenues. The overriding objective was to reduce net migration. In January 2011 it was reported that the Immigration Department was forecasting a reduction in the annual rate of student arrivals from 134,700 in March 2010 to 64,500 by June 2014 (Trounson, 2011). In June 2011 the federal Immigration Minister, Chris Bowen, told a conference in Sydney that the student visa programme had to change. 'I want more students to come here for a range of economic, foreign affairs and educational reasons', stated Bowen. 'But it is important that students come here for education purposes and not in search of a migration outcome.... The increase in student numbers is what led most directly to the increase in the net overseas migration rate topping 300,000 a year, which was unsustainable' (quoted in Bennett, 2011, p 4). While tertiary institutions still had a strong economic incentive to recruit international students, Australia's total number of international students, and its share of the global student market, was destined to fall significantly.

Australian Education International data showed that in the period November 2009 to November 2010 the number of commencing students was 9.3 per cent less than in the period November 2008 to November 2009. There was a 21.3 per cent fall in English language colleges and 8.2 per cent in VET. At that stage higher education numbers were still rising, having increased by 2.4 per cent (Trounson, 2011), and the decline mostly affected students from India. Total commencements into higher education from India fell from 12,551 in 2008 to 11,336 in 2009 and 5,756 in 2010 (Deloitte Access Economics, 2011, p 12). However, the decline was beginning to spread to other source countries. In 2009-10 student visas for higher education and postgraduate research declined by 10.2 per cent compared to the previous year (Deloitte Access Economics, 2011, p 15). In March 2011 offshore visa applications were 20 per cent lower than a year earlier. The number of applications for student visas for higher education in Australia was down 66 per cent from India and 20 per cent from China. The corresponding figures for vocational education were 93 per cent for India and 65 per cent for China (Ross, 2011). In China, where the number of students going to the US continued to increase, student recruitment agencies highlighted the required financial support and changes to the permanent residency requirements as key factors in a decline in applications for student visas for Australia (Sainsbury, 2011).

A report by Deloitte Access Economics for Universities Australia estimated that in 2011 international student commencements into higher education would fall by 23 per cent and total student numbers by 11 per cent, with a corresponding drop in the revenues received in international student fees. The decline was expected to continue into 2012 (Deloitte Access Economics, 2011, pp iii, vii). In the first nine months of 2010-11 export earnings were one billion dollars lower than in the corresponding period of 2009-10 (ABS, 2011).

Undoing the changes

It was widely expected that the number of international students in higher education, where many public institutions were highly dependent on the export market, would fall by at least a third over the next three years. The federal government was faced with the potential for large-scale collapse in institutional income and political pressures to reverse its tight fiscal policy so as to bail out the universities. With fiscal considerations even more important than sustaining a low-to-medium position on migration, in December 2010 the government asked a former state politician, Michael Knight, to review the student visa programme.

The Knight (2011) review reported in June 2011, although the federal government digested its report for three months before release. Its proposals, which were all accepted by the federal government, signified a return to a more student-friendly policy, with the inevitable corollary of a more migration-friendly policy as well. It applied the changes in policy and regulation only to universities, where there had been fewer problems of sham education and migration-driven course profiles, and there were stronger administrative systems for self-regulation, but it was expected that the changes would be later extended to selected VET providers as well. All provisions concerning demonstrated financial support were dropped. Visa processing was to be sped up, although this provision was to be implemented slowly because of staffing restrictions.

Individual universities were given enhanced responsibility to ensure students were bona fide, with the warning that if self-regulation failed, they would be taken off the list of preferred providers and more stringent conditions on student support and visa checks would be imposed. Students gained more flexible work rights, and international student graduates were provided with a new post-study work visa that enabled them to work for two to four years after graduation, depending on the level of the course. The last was a most significant change that signalled a renewed commitment to the global competition for mobile skilled labour and lifted Australia's positioning in relation to competition from the other English-speaking countries.

Problems and prospects

International education will continue to expand at the global level because of the expected growth of urban middle-class populations, especially in East, South and Southeast Asia. One estimate is that the global middle class will grow to a level of two billion between 2010 and 2030, tripling in size. The World Bank suggests there will be 20 million more middle-class people in Malaysia, 50 million in Indonesia and up to 800 million in China (Murray, 2011, p 11). Most of the new middle-class families will be educated in domestic tertiary education systems. But regardless of the quantity and quality of domestic provision and the precise trajectories of participation rates in the emerging economies, a minority of middle-class families will continue to use international education, as before, because it provides both career and migration opportunities. Rapid growth of the globally mobile student population will continue. The question, however, is *which* exporting nations will provide for the increased student numbers, and in particular, whether Australia and New Zealand will continue to 'punch above their weight' in the international education market.

For Australia a return to the 2010-11 regime in migration policy would mean international student numbers would continue to fall and the nation would lose market share. A relatively high Australian dollar compounded this by weakening export competitiveness. Deloitte Access Economics (2011) found that the strengthening dollar had not been a major factor in driving down numbers – 'international student commencements in Australia appear only loosely correlated with movements in the Australian dollar' (p 29) – but could inhibit the recovery of Australia's export position, for example, with respect to China. Following the changes instigated by the Knight (2011) review, at least a partial recovery is in prospect. It is unclear whether the previous rates of export growth will return, although at institutional level there are still strong incentives to expand supply because government funding remains depressed.

Export sector in New Zealand

The New Zealand Education Act 1989 empowered the nation's state institutions to charge fees and thereby launched the New Zealand export sector. In 1998 Education New Zealand was formed to coordinate, advocate and resource the industry at home and abroad (Smith and Rae, 2006, p 28). The industry is about one sixth the size of that of Australia. In 2010 there were 916 New Zealand institutions providing full-fee education to international students, including eight universities, 20 polytechnics and 246 other tertiary providers, mostly private institutions. The other providers were schools, mostly with small international student populations, averaging 26 students per school. The universities enrolled 19,350 full fee-paying students, polytechnics 11,414 students, other tertiary institutions, which included foundation programmes and English language colleges, 48,163 students, and schools 16,064 students. The eight universities enrolled an average of 2,460 students, polytechnics 587. There were 98,474 students in 2010, a 3 per cent increase on 2009. Students were overwhelmingly concentrated in two areas, the Auckland region (58 per cent) and the Canterbury region that included Christchurch (15 per cent) (ENZ, 2011).

In total international education generated NZD$708.6 million in tuition revenues, including $284.0 million in the universities, $77.0 million in the polytechnics and $198.1 million in the private tertiary sector. On top of this international students spent in many areas such as transport, accommodation, food and entertainment, generating further economic activity. The average tuition fee was $19,793 in the universities, $13,090 in the polytechnics and $10,746 in the private tertiary institutions (ENZ, 2011). The total economic impact was calculated at $2.1 billion in 2007-08, compared to tuition revenues that year of $597 million. There were offshore earnings of $70 million that year (MOENZ, 2011b, p 17). Note, however, that this was below the export earnings at the peak of the industry in 2003, which totalled $2.3 billion (Smith and Rae, 2006, p 27). Again, valued in current prices at $2.3 billion in June 2008 – albeit after five years of inflation – education was the nation's fifth largest export earner that year, after dairy ($8.8 billion), tourism ($8.8 billion), meat ($4.6 billion) and mineral fuels ($2.6 billion) (ENZ, 2011).

In total 47 per cent of all students in tertiary education were enrolled in programmes offering English to speakers of other languages. There was variation between nations, in the sectors of educational enrolment. Compared to overall averages, students from China, Malaysia and the US were over-represented in universities, Korean students in schools, students from India in vocational training, and students from Japan and Korea in English language programmes (ENZ, 2011). Table 4.5 provides data on the top 15 source nations for students.

Table 4.5: Nations of origin of international students in New Zealand, all sectors and universities, top 15 nations

Nation of student origin	Students in all sectors of education		Students in universities only			
(importing nation)	2009	2010	2009	2010	Change 2009-10 %	Proportion of students 2010 %
China[1]	21,327	21,258	6,086	5,864	−3.6	29.8
Korea	16,070	15,282	1,253	1,279	2.0	6.5
India	9,252	11,597	1,140	1,240	8.8	6.3
Japan	9,761	9,745	857	971	13.3	4.9
Saudi Arabia	5,445	5,455	1,215	1,245	2.5	6.3
Germany	3,622	3,905	357	432	21.0	2.2
Thailand	3,098	3,387	378	302	−20.1	1.5
Brazil	3,020	3,109	41	46	12.2	0.2
United States	2,296	2,373	2,018	2,115	4.8	10.7
Malaysia	2,150	2,133	1,666	1,717	3.1	8.7
Taiwan China	1,848	1,967	315	323	2.5	1.6
Vietnam	1,527	1,909	441	551	24.9	2.8
France[2]	1,792	1,901	108	141	30.6	0.7
Fiji	1,304	1,246	na	na	na	na
Switzerland	1,366	1,241	21	21	0	0.1
All nations	95,524	98,474	19,424	19,678	1.3	100.0

Notes: [1] Includes Hong Kong SAR. [2] Includes French territories in the Pacific. na = data not available.

Source: ENZ (2011); MOENZ (2011)

The New Zealand export industry has been characterised by both rapid growth and fluctuation. OECD data show that in 2008 the number of foreign students in New Zealand was at seven times the level of the year 2000, a period in which numbers doubled in Australia (OECD, 2011, p 316). The principal importers were China, Korea, India and Japan. However, growth was not consistent, and entry from China rose and fell sharply in the middle years of the decade. Figure 4.2, using New Zealand government data, shows the longer-term trends in total students, and students from China.

As discussed in Chapter One, in 2003 Chinese Embassy officials advised the New Zealand government in Wellington that they were

Figure 4.2: Enrolments of international students in all institutions, public tertiary education institutions, and from China in all institutions, New Zealand, 2000-10

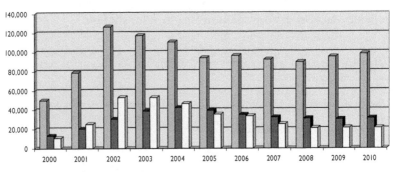

☐ Enrolments all institutions ■ Enrolments public tertiary institutions ☐ Enrolments all institutions, students from China¹

Note: * From 2006 onwards only, enrolments from China include Hong Kong SAR. Student enrolments from Hong Kong constituted about 2 per cent of total China enrolments in 2005.

Source: MOENZ (2007, 2011b)

dissatisfied with the level and quality of the attention given to the safety of Chinese students studying there (Li, 2007). China was concerned about the licence allowed fraudulent suppliers, the racial vilification of some Asian people in New Zealand, and hostile media coverage, and the number of Chinese students who became victims and/or perpetrators of crime. The New Zealand government's response rested largely on reference to the Pastoral Care Code, the central regulatory instrument.

Commencements from China dropped sharply in response. As Chinese students were the largest single element of the international student population, this sent the industry into decline. This first affected private sector colleges but then spread to public tertiary institutions. In 2004 there were 29,821 international students enrolled in universities, but this fell to 21,748 by 2007 and still further to 19,678 by 2010 (MOENZ, 2011b, p 3). Table 4.6 summarises the trend.

The main decline in numbers was at diploma and first-degree levels. Postgraduate enrolments rose from 4,638 in 2004 to 7,721 in 2010. 'This increase can partly be attributed to the success of the "domestic fees status for new international PhD students" policy introduced from 2006' (MOENZ, 2011b, p 11).

Between 2004 and 2010 the number of approved visas granted to Chinese students dropped from 55,937 to 22,799, a decline of 57 per cent (MOENZ, 2011b, p 6). Table 4.7 indicates the trends in the number of students from the leading four source countries over the 2006-10 period. Total students from China fell by 36.8 per cent between 2006 and 2010 and those from Japan fell by 31.8 per cent over the same period. There was also fluctuation in relation to Korea. However, student numbers from India rose significantly.

Problems and prospects

Table 4.6: Enrolment of international students in universities and polytechnics, New Zealand, 2004-10

Sector	2004	2005	2006	2007	2008	2009	2010
Universities	29,821	27,640	24,540	21,748	19,562	19,424	19,678
Polytechnics	12,599	11,965	10,721	10,625	10,586	10,994	11,740

Source: MOENZ (2011b)

Table 4.7: Number of international fee-paying students in all sectors of education in New Zealand, 2006-10

Nation of student origin (importing nation)	2006	2007	2008	2009	2010	Change 2006-10 %
China[1]	33,649	25,216	21,080	21,327	21,258	−36.8
Korea	15,930	17,500	17,331	16,070	15,282	−4.1
India	2,599	3,855	6,348	9,252	11,597	356.2
Japan	14,299	12,325	10,755	9,761	9,745	−31.8
All students	96,583	92,502	90,082	95,524	98,474	2.0

Note: [1] Includes Hong Kong SAR.

Source: ENZ (2011)

The fortunes of New Zealand in international education, like those of Australia, are tied to the Asian source countries that provide more than four fifths of all students. Demand appears to be more volatile than for Australia, and more influenced by reputational factors, as suggested by the drop in numbers from China after 2003. The decline in the number of international students entering Australia after 2009 was affected by reputational considerations to some extent – primarily in relation to India – but was primarily driven by the reduction in the supply of student visas and in migration opportunities for graduates. Australia appears to be in a stronger position in the long term. While both nations are affected by perceptions that the quality of their programmes is inferior to that of the UK and the US, Australia offers a larger set of employment and career opportunities and its best research universities are stronger than those of New Zealand. The comparative assets enjoyed by both countries – openness, relatively safe and peaceful civil environments, recreational opportunities, and a cost of living cheaper than those applying in the US and UK – are similar.

At the end of the 2000s in New Zealand numbers from India rose to compensate for declines from East Asia, but there was no guarantee that this would always be the case. The importance of reputational factors in the New Zealand industry draws attention to the potential of the distinctive New Zealand system of regulation to play into the level of foreign demand for the nation's education. This is discussed further in Chapter Six.

Conclusion: markets and regulation

Australia and New Zealand are major players in the global market for cross-border education. Both have experienced ups and downs in market share, which should be considered minor in economic terms. The longer-term trend is upward. New Zealand experienced greater growth over the last decade, having begun from a significantly lower base and being a later starter in the international race than its neighbour across the Tasman Sea. Overall, both industries are economically secure despite policy changes and in the case of New Zealand, engineered fluctuations in demand, which have constituted partial interruptions.

Market strategy matters to regulation, and in particular it affects the overall direction of the regime, as Chapters Five and Six reveal in relation to both countries. The converse is also true, with regulation affecting the opportunities and challenges faced by institutions and the national education sector as a whole (Marginson, 2005). With market prospects for the future of the two countries likely to be sustainable, at least in the narrow economic sense – given especially more of the same projected growth in the numbers of the middle class across neighbouring Asia – regulation will continue to be challenged by, and traded off against, questions of student wellbeing. It is to such questions that the analysis now turns.

FIVE

Much regulation, minimal protection: the Australian model

Introduction

The Australian model of international student welfare regulation has more formal provisions than almost all others. It has a more extensive body of legislation dealing directly with international higher education than comparable Anglo common law countries, such as the UK and the US, and it has an accompanying set of regulations guiding educational providers. Australia is a signatory to GATS, thus bearing (albeit loose) connections to international instruments. There are also extensive rules on migration through education, which continue to evolve to the time of writing, conventions governing the provision of trans-national education, quality assurance mechanisms and individual legal provisions operating at the local level. The Australian government has also introduced an independent arbiter specific to international education to hear student grievances unresolved at institution level – in legal expression, an ombudsman existing within and as a branch of the Commonwealth ombudsman that handles complaints by vocational college students. Finally, Australia has legislation and accompanying formal regulations specifically applied to higher and vocational education together, incorporating student consumer protection and limited pastoral care rights provisions. These take the form of the ESOS Act and the National Code, together commonly referred to as the 'ESOS Framework'.

The objective of this chapter is to interrogate the Australian regulation regime, examining the formal mechanisms using existing literature and key documents, and primary data from students whose home countries are from all over the world, although in the great majority of cases from Asia. The students whose views are discussed in data analysis are enrolled in nine Australian universities and represent a range of regions and sub-sectors across the country. However, interviews with staff from universities and the relevant national policy portfolios provide the basis for the more extensive analysis, supplementing the student data by uncovering the rationales behind, and the gaps within, the formal regulation sphere. This approach allows for the induction of insights into the informal sphere, which, we argue, is the more deterministic despite the extensive formal provisions.

Analysis of the interview data leads directly to the central finding of the chapter, that despite the extensive codification underpinning the ESOS Framework, the regulation of international student welfare is largely non-specific and mainly non-binding in effect. In that sense, in welfare terms Australia is largely a regime of implicit regulation, although as discussed in Chapter Two, regulation theory suggests that this *is* regulation never the less. Accordingly, student local and transnational networks, and social and family connections, are key to the determination of general wellbeing, and the absence of specific and effectively enforceable formal protections highlights a national welfare deficit that is internationally significant.

The first section of this chapter outlines the legal context of student welfare by discussing individual legal provisions governing international education in Australia. The second section overviews the ESOS Act and the National Code, with an emphasis on welfare aspects. The third section explores the continuing debate on the regulatory contours of student welfare. The fourth section analyses the role of the informal welfare sphere.

The higher education law context: individual legal provisions

As is the case for other countries, in Australia the literature on education law is sparse. Two main works in the area have been released within the last 15 years: Ramsay and Shorten's (1996) *Education and the law* and Jackson and Varnham's (2007) *Law for educators*. The latter, more recent and thus more applicable here, makes clear that '[t]here was a time when the words 'students' and 'law' would not be heard in the same sentence' (p vii). Yet, like Ramsay and Shorten, they concede that this situation has gradually been changing, to the point that Australia, along with New Zealand, now has perhaps the most extensive body of code covering students of any country in the world. Similarly to the US and UK models the Australian regime incorporates specific individual rules, both legal and pseudo-legal.

Most provisions covered here are federal, although state law also features.[1] All public universities – that is, almost all universities – are regulated by state Acts of Parliament, each under a distinct piece of legislation. The exception is the Australian National University, which was created in the Australian Capital Territory by the Commonwealth government. Although most were created by their relevant Act, not all were. For example, the private Australian Catholic University is a company incorporated under Victorian corporations law, and the private Bond University is actually a collection of companies established under the Companies (Queensland) Code and further subject to the Bond University Act of 1987 (Queensland). The private Notre Dame University, on the other hand, while having a similar legal status, exists under Western Australian corporations law and is a public university. In a purely legal analysis, therefore, understanding the rights of students in universities engages constitutional and corporate law issues.

In practice Australian universities are subject to a combination of state and Commonwealth laws, with increasing influence from the federal sphere since the Commonwealth took over their funding in the 1950s. Despite federal funding, however, they are subject to state-level audits. There is an ongoing struggle between the states and the Commonwealth for greater control of the sector, and both sets of laws apply, although in ways that are legally complex and controversial. For example, the Commonwealth may seek to regulate universities through funding, and through its 'defence' and 'foreign corporations' powers (Jackson and Varnham, 2007, Section 2.2), but its control is indirect. As argued later in this chapter, this and other issues of legal federalism influence staff interviewees' perceptions of the possibilities for formalising student welfare provisions.

Universities each have individual or organisation-level governance frameworks, usually incorporating a 'council' to whom the vice-chancellor (equivalent to the chief executive officer) reports, and a senior academic body usually known as the 'academic board'. Such arrangements can affect student academic and non-academic life opportunities. Students are 'members' of a university and as such have members' rights. Although university Acts are usually largely silent on members' rights, membership under company law applies, such that students (and staff) have the right: not to be arbitrarily dismissed from membership; not to be oppressed; to insist that the university act according to the law; and to insist that those in charge of the university do not perpetrate a fraud on the membership (Section 2.10). In addition and in effect, students (and staff) are entitled to criticise or otherwise express opinions about the university without loss of membership.

Students have recourse to internal and external means of redress if they feel that their rights may have been violated. Traditional arrangements in the UK involved a university 'visitor' as internal adjudicator, although this has had limited purchase in Australia and has been found to be largely ineffective (Jackson and Varnham, 2007, Section 2.10). On the other hand, as discussed further on in this chapter, there has been an increase in universities adopting internal student ombudsmen and more effective grievance mechanisms (Stuhmcke, 2001; Astor, 2005), and there are a variety of external administrative appeals mechanisms (Section 2.10). Students also have rights under contract law in ways similar to those outlined in relation to the US and the UK in Chapter Two. For example, in the trans-national education arena universities may be liable to students through their partner or subsidiary provider offshore or onshore (Section 2.13).

Quality assurance is an area of regulation well established in Australia and internationally (see, for example, Daniel, 2002; Uvalic-Trumbic, 2002; van Damme, 2002). In March 2000, with the creation of Australia's Ministerial Council on Education, Employment, Training and Youth Affairs (MCEETYA), state and federal education ministers released the National Protocols for Higher Education Approval Processes (the National Protocols). These were administered by the Australian Universities Quality Agency (AUQA), 'an independent, not-for-profit national agency that promotes, audits, and reports on quality assurance in Australian higher education' (AUQA, 2010). AUQA was – and its successor body TEQSA (Tertiary Education Quality and Standards Agency) remains – owned and funded by the ministers, but formally stands independent of the government, having responsibility for quality audits of higher education institutions and accreditation authorities. It reports on university performance and outcomes, provides advice on quality enhancement and assurance, and liaises with quality assurance bodies in other countries. It also has responsibility for ensuring that the overseas teaching operations of Australian institutions adhere to domestic quality standards (Sections 2.14-2.18). Accreditation of providers and courses is also regulated by the Australian Qualifications Framework (AQF, 2010), which in turn liaises with the country's migration authorities in decisions relating to qualifications and occupations consistent with skills needs and shortages. This, as argued below in the interview data analysis, has raised significant welfare issues for some students.

The financing of Australian universities is regulated by the Higher Education Support Act (Commonwealth) 2003 (HESA) and the associated HESA guidelines for the Commonwealth Grants Scheme, with quality and accountability requirements, fairness requirements with respect to the application of 'merit' principles (Section 2.18) and student assistance provisions in relation to student higher education charges (Section 2.29). In addition, discrimination laws are applicable to universities and applied differently across the states (Sections 3.2-

3.10). Intellectual property provisions are mainly federal (Sections 3.12-3.15), and freedom of information mainly state-based (Sections 3.16-3.17). Students also have rights under the law of torts in relation to negligence (Sections13.2-13.9), under the law of contract in relation to a university's potential liability for educational outcomes (Sections 13.10-13.12). Consumer protection provisions, which are covered in the next section under the discussion of the ESOS Framework, are also regulated by the Trade Practices Act 1974 (Commonwealth) (Section 13.13), including recognition of the 'financial inequality' between student and university (Section 13.15) and what students may claim in cases they challenge under the Act.

Finally, as in the US and the UK, Australian universities are regulated under laws dealing with freedom of expression (Sections 14.1-14.7) and privacy of information (Sections 14.9-14.19) as well as the employment of academics (Sections 16.1-16.17) and academic freedom (Sections 16.18-16.25). In principle all of these have a bearing on student lives.

The ESOS Act and the National Code: the ESOS Framework

Specifically in relation to international students, and to consumer protection and pastoral care, formal regulation in Australia is channelled through the Education Services for Overseas Students Act (or ESOS Act) of 2000 and the *National code of practice for registration authorities and training to overseas students* (or the National Code) of 2001 (and revised in 2007; see: DEST, 2007a, 2007b). At its base the ESOS Act specifies requirements that universities and non-university higher education institutions must meet in order to be registered as higher education providers (jointly referred to as 'providers'). Provisions are designed to protect students by requiring that providers do not engage in 'misleading or deceptive conduct' (Part 3, Division 1, Section 15) and that they 'refund course money' in circumstances where courses 'do not commence on the agreed starting date' (Part 3.2.27.3). Separate clauses cover cases of student default on payment of course money (Part 3.2.28).

These protections are backed by the ESOS Assurance Fund, to which providers must contribute each year. The Fund exists to compensate students in the case of promised courses not being offered, such that 'students are provided with suitable alternative courses, or have their course money refunded if the provider cannot provide the courses that the students have paid for' (Part 5). In addition, the Act prescribes a variety of rights and responsibilities for providers, particularly in relation to fund contributions (Part 5.4), general enforcement of the Act's terms and conditions, monitoring of providers and sanctions in case of their non-compliance (Parts 6 and 7).

Although students are afforded rights as consumers of 'quality' education under the Act, it is the National Code that explicates the substance of these rights. Established in 2001 under the ESOS Act (Part 4) and revised in 2007 (DEST, 2007b), the Code supports the Act in two ways: first, by specifying pre-conditions for registration of providers; and second, by 'establish[ing] and safeguard[ing] Australia's reputation as a provider of high quality education and training.' It addresses quality and national reputation by imposing nationally consistent cross-border education standards and by providing 'student welfare and support services' and 'nationally consistent standards for dealing with student complaints and appeals' (DEST, 2007b, Part A.3.1). Given their centrality to the issue of student entitlements, these require slight elaboration.

Where students are under 18 years of age, the Australian government must be satisfied that appropriate arrangements are in place for student accommodation, support and general welfare arrangements during the whole of the period that they are under 18 and studying onshore (Standard 5). Yet accommodation and living arrangements are the only specified requirements (Standards 5.1.a–5.1.d, 5.2, 5.3.a), with 'support and general welfare arrangements' being mentioned but left largely undefined. Where students are over 18 (Standard 6), the requirements of providers are even less specific, prescribing that they must provide access to support services and orientation programmes, with student access being given to university staff who assess and administer these. In addition institutions must have 'critical incident policies' in place for all students (also Standard 6), with a critical incident defined by the Department of Education, Science and Training (DEST) as 'a traumatic event, or the threat of such (within or outside Australia), which causes extreme stress, fear or injury.' Although each provider must have a critical incident policy on hand and in writing, notably '[t]he details of your [the provider's] Critical Incident Policy do not need to be shared with students at orientation' (DEST, 2007c).

Students both under and over 18 do not enjoy stringent legal enforcement and appeals mechanisms guaranteeing protections. Crucially, under Standard 8 of the Code providers are required only to offer students '*internal*' processes for handling complaints and appeals, and where students request independent mechanisms, these are appointed and called on by the provider and not by the student (Standard 8). This is particularly problematic when it is considered in addition that the Code prescribes student compliance mechanisms with visa conditions and handles complaints by providers against student breaches of their visas (Part A.3.1.d). In this way students are subject to somewhat rigidly enforceable compliance but only loosely enforceable protections.

Changes to the ESOS Act made effective in February 2010, reflected in the ESOS Amendment (Re-registration of Providers and Other Measures) Act, went some way towards enhancing protection for some students, although mainly by providing more consumer rights. The changes were designed to protect and enhance Australia's educational reputation for international marketing purposes, while in the process also constraining the aggregate supply of student visas, making it more difficult for international graduates of Australian universities to gain permanent resident status and/or to migrate to the country (see Chapter Four, this volume). The central changes relevant to the discussion in this chapter were as follows. All institutions currently registered under the Commonwealth Register of Institutions and Courses for Overseas Students (CRICOS) had to undergo re-registration by the end of calendar 2010. This was to ensure that the government furnishes (at least a market perception) that the right to be, and to continue to be, a provider only extended to reputable providers. There were other new registration requirements. First, the primary purpose of the provider had to be shown to be education and not any other business. Second, the provider had to demonstrate the capacity to provide education of a standard deemed to be of sufficient quality. Finally, providers had to provide a list of the education agents who represented them and promoted their services to prospective international students. As noted, these requirements responded to a growing awareness of vocational education colleges that were sub-standard in quality or working in areas of marginal need, and operating primarily as routes into migration rather than training institutions.

In allied changes the conditions imposed by states and territories on education providers were recognised by the Commonwealth. The definition of 'suitable alternative course' – which applied when students were forced by provider closure to withdraw from the course – now had to be further clarified by the provider. There was also a requirement that the provider furnish the ESOS assurance manager with a report, within 60 days of provider closure, of the number of students affected by closure and the amount of money claimed from the Assurance Fund. Finally, a 'designated authority' had to use a risk management approach when considering matters relating to the potential or prospective re-registration of a provider.

Regulatory debate

The emphases of these changes to ESOS lay squarely on the protection of funds invested by the student in enrolling in their chosen course, and on ensuring that international market perceptions of Australian providers were not diminished by revelations of potentially sub-standard courses provided mainly by vocational colleges. Welfare considerations were thin on the ground. Yet the wellbeing of students was not entirely absent from public debate. As controversy can be a catalyst for regulatory change, the debate is worthy of consideration.

Amid the gradual downgrading in the share of funding by government, and the continual rush to market international education globally – and given that education has been among the nation's top exports for the better part of the last decade – a debate has emerged as to whether the Australian economy and education providers have become too reliant on the international dollar. In a similar market context education and provider quality concerns have been raised in relation to the growth in international vocational education and training, given the close nexus that has developed between the nation's skills needs, vocational training agenda and immigration (Birrell, 2009). On the other side of the coin, downturns in enrolment numbers in the sector have been partly due to the most recent appreciation in the exchange rate, but more so to regulatory changes discussed in Chapter Four earlier. These have sparked widespread concern over declining revenues and student numbers (Ross, 2009; Birrell and Smith, 2010).

Quality assurance has been keenly debated in the same context (Hare, 2010), and issues of the broader social and cultural benefits have been highlighted (Davis, 2010). More explicit aspects of student welfare in general have been put into question (Wesley, 2009; Marginson et al, 2010), including housing and accommodation and in particular whether universities can do more directly to provide international student residences (Spence, 2010). Perhaps the most highly publicised issues – and potentially the issues most damaging to Australia's international market share – are those concerning student safety and crime, most notably in recent years in relation to highly publicised racist attacks against Indian students (Nyland et al, 2010; Woodward, 2010).

These issues have led directly into key government-sponsored inquiries and public policy discussion documents.

Government inquiries

Inquiries sponsored by government in recent years have recommended important changes in international education, some of which have been accepted by government. Chaired by former Commonwealth Minister Bruce Baird, the *Review of the Education Services for Overseas Students (ESOS) Act 2000* recommended changes that resulted in the amendments described in the preceding discussion (Australian Government, 2010). Baird urged that ESOS be made 'stronger' by toughening sanctions against non-compliant providers and by seeking to ensure that government 'resourcing for regulatory activities' is adequate (Recommendation 5). He also argued that regulation should be 'simpler', principally through each provider having only a single regulator to whom it was responsible for reporting purposes (Recommendation 6). Finally, ESOS should be made 'smarter' by giving the Commonwealth Education Minister more direct oversight and delegated powers over providers in order to ensure the consistent application of the Act across the board nationally (Recommendation 7).

Importantly, and as discussed further below, to the mantra of 'smarter' Baird added that those students who thus far, in cases of their dissatisfaction with provider decisions, had had no effective access to an independent complaints body, should be given the right to appeal to a newly created international education arm of the Commonwealth ombudsman (Recommendation 8). This – since the adoption and resultant establishment of the international student ombudsman – now applies, although only to students of private vocational education and training colleges, given that students enrolled in *higher* education providers have already enjoyed access to state-level ombudsmen. Importantly, however, state ombudsmen are not and were not, in any obvious way to students, designed as education-specific bodies or even as bodies domiciled as avenues for international student grievances.

Seeing the need to reform the connection between education, migration and the skills needs of the national economy, Baird also recommended the amendment of the Migration Act to enable more flexible approaches in cases of potential visa cancellation (Recommendation 9). Finally, Baird recommended 'safeguarding students' [financial] interests' (Recommendations 16-19), emphasising in particular the need to establish a single 'tuition protection service'. Effectively this suggestion was designed to place greater responsibilities on 'higher risk providers', in the process also harmonising tuition protection arrangements for domestic and international students.

In a significantly broader *Review of Australian higher education*, the 'Bradley Review' (Australian Government, 2008), as it became known, had earlier been commissioned to interrogate the question of whether the nation's higher education system 'is structured, organised and financed to position Australia to compete effectively in the new globalised economy.' The investigative panel, chaired by Professor Denise Bradley – after whom the report became named – emphasised (p xi) that Australia was falling behind internationally in performance and investment in higher education, given the important finding (OECD, 2008) that it was the only country within the developed world to have travelled backwards in public expenditure on higher education during the previous decade, under the Howard Liberal/National Coalition government. For the Bradley Review another pressure for reform came from the need for a greater social inclusion agenda within the higher education system in order to simultaneously address the social equity and skills and knowledge needs of the nation (Australian Government, 2008, p xi). The Review cited in particular the need to provide the benefits of a tertiary education to a wider aggregate number of students, and as part of that, students from a wider range of socioeconomic backgrounds and circumstances.

For Bradley and her colleagues the role of the *international* education sector within the recommended change process was vital, and Australia was well placed, they argued, to harness change processes given that it was well down the path, and indeed was an early leader in, the internationalisation and massification processes beginning in the 1980s. Further to a response to the growth of international education as an export the Review recommended that the regulatory and other functions of Australian Education International be separated, with the former to be taken by a new, independent national regulator (Recommendation 11). This proposal was adopted in 2010. To assist international students enrolled in research degrees in areas of skills shortage the Review also recommended the provision of up to 1,000 tuition subsidy scholarships per year (Recommendation 13). In a more controversial recommendation it also suggested (Recommendation 14) that providers use a proportion of their international student income for research students, so as to provide financial assistance to meet living expenses for international research degree students, thereby matching the proposed Australian government tuition scholarships. Other financial incentives affecting the same category of student lay in Recommendation 15, that the Commonwealth government 'liaise with the States and Territories to ensure consistent policies for school fee waivers for the dependents of international research students in government-subsidised places.' It was also suggested that conditions for spouse work visas should be improved.

Other recommendations that related to student welfare included those concerning quality assurance and accreditation (Recommendations 19-24, 43). In their relation to international education these proposals were largely consistent with the Baird Review, as were the recommendations relating to the vocational education sector (Recommendations 44-46).

Proceeding in parallel with the ESOS and higher education reviews was the Council of Australian Governments' (COAG) *International student strategy* and the associated *International student roundtable*, designed 'to improve the experience of international students in Australia and in turn benefit all of Australian society' (COAG, 2009). Perhaps recognising that unfettered growth without re-regulation may be harmful to students and broader society in the long term, the strategy sought 'to place Australia's international education on a more sustainable basis.' It proposed to improve pre- and post-arrival information for students and increase engagement with the wider community on matters of international education; promote 'cultural understanding, tolerance and language skills'; change the relationship between international education and migration; and attend to the quality of education providers.

Other government inquiries have similarly explored a range of student welfare issues, although none more deeply than the question of whether Australia needs an independent adjudicator devoted specifically to international education, outside and independent of the providers.

The question of an education ombudsman

From a student wellbeing perspective, one of the factors separating Australia from New Zealand, and indeed the UK, is the existence in the other two countries of an independent student complaints and appeals body. The UK has an Office of the Independent Adjudicator in Higher Education (OIA), an independent national ombudsman-like tribunal that allows for student rights to be mediated on by means of legal and pseudo-legal grievance handling and enforcement by a party outside the student–institution relationship. This has a similar philosophy and mission to its New Zealand counterpart, the IEAA, but applies only to higher education and thus excludes the vocational sector.

The student grievance regime in Australia consists of internal or institution-specific procedures initiated by the student and most often channelled through internal higher education provider or VET college student ombudsman and/or internal dean of students, and the largely non-specific external mechanisms offered through the ESOS Framework. Under Standard 8 of the National Code – 'Complaints and appeals' – it is stipulated that the registered provider must have 'an appropriate internal complaints and handling and appeals process' (Standard 8.1). The provider must have 'arrangements in place for a person or body independent of and external to the registered provider' (Standard 8.2). Yet no particular external body or person is specified and in practice, students for this purpose have accessed their agent/ representative, legal advice and/or the services of bodies such as the state ombudsman or the Migration Review Tribunal, depending on the nature of the grievance. If the student is not satisfied with the conduct or the outcome of the internal process and wishes to take the matter to an external party, under the National Code the provider 'must advise the student of his or her right to access the external appeals process at minimal or no cost', and maintain his/her enrolment while the grievance process is ongoing (Standard 8.3) (DEST, 2007b, p 18). There is no independent, national-level, education- or international education-specific grievance handling body, or ombudsman.

The need to examine the viability of such a body in Australia is underlined by the increasing number of students taking grievances to external, non-education tribunals, mainly state ombudsmen (Stuhmcke, 2001; Astor, 2005). In 2005 seven of the eight public law ombudsmen wrote an open letter to the national newspaper, *The Australian*, to express their concern that *student* grievances received had increased and that educational institutions were less than competent at internal complaints handling. This is despite a simultaneous increase in the creation of new internal institution student complaints procedures and officers such as internal student ombudsmen and deans of students (Olliffe and Stuhmcke, 2007, p 204).

The quest to identify a regulatory voice other than government and the institutions has been given a fillip by tragic incidences of public violence committed on international students from Asia in general but India more specifically (see, in particular, Nyland et al, 2010). In all likelihood there is little potential to avoid such incidents without an overhaul of broader accompanying policy spheres such as criminal justice and policing, and of the existence of racism. Also, an ombudsman would not be given the power to address such problems, at least not alone. Yet an ombudsman can contribute to the broader milieu of independence in the search for justice.

As noted in Chapter Five, other drivers include revelations of dishonest practices by migration agents seeking to recruit international students using misleading information on job prospects on graduation from Australian courses, particularly in the VET sector. There have been concerns among both students and policy makers that a minority of VET colleges have also either delivered courses of less than advertised standards or have not delivered courses and/or have failed to reimburse students for fees paid after college financial failure (Baird, 2009, pp 8-9).

In the face of these developments, and with general and wide-ranging student welfare concerns (Marginson et al, 2010), a policy literature has been taking shape. The Australian Learning and Teaching Council has investigated the viability of a higher education student ombudsman as one reform option, although it did not commit to the concept on the grounds that 'there should be more focus on improving university internal systems' and that an ombudsman may 'just add another layer to already complex range of external forums for redress' (Jackson et al, 2009, pp 2-3). There was little or no actual analysis of the appropriate mix of internal and external means. The 2009 COAG *International student strategy* and *International student roundtable* (COAG, 2009) did not resolve the question of an ombudsman; indeed it not deal with the question. However, using similar justifications to those relied on by the Baird report, the federal Parliament's Senate Standing Committee on Education, Employment and Workplace Relations recommended that 'the jurisdiction of the Commonwealth Ombudsman be extended to cover the international education sector' (Australian Government, 2009, p 2). It was that Committee's model that was subsequently implemented, as part of the 2010 changes discussed above.

However, the government has resisted the recommendation to install an education-specific body covering university students, although as noted, two of Australia's international education competitors, New Zealand and the UK, have adopted national ombudsman models in response to student welfare and education dispute resolution concerns. There are differences between these two models. The New Zealand case will be discussed in detail in Chapter Six. The UK OIA is funded by compulsory contributions from institutions. It is a company limited by guarantee operating only in England and Wales. International students in Scotland and Northern Ireland do not have access to the OIA, nor to a comparable body (Harris, 2007; Olliffe and Stuhmcke, 2007, p 208). The OIA hears cases using similar procedures and principles to New Zealand's IEAA. Yet the IEAA is legitimised by institutions' understandable desire for ongoing registration under the Pastoral Care Code, and the IEAA has the power to de-register an institution from the Code if the institution does not comply with a ruling. The OIA in the UK, on the other hand, is not backed by a code, and the legal powers of the OIA are less water-tight, given that its rulings are recommendatory and are not strictly to 'order' a provider to take or refrain from taking a particular remedial action.

As the OIA's rules make clear (Section 7.7), 'any non-compliance ... with a Recommendation will be reported to the [OIA] Board and publicised in the [OIA] Annual Report'. As Harris (2007, p 586) suggests, while this is not strictly compulsion, there is in practice a strong pressure for compliance. The public relations implications for the provider flowing from non-compliance with an OIA decision are such that compliance is highly likely. The OIA's formal independence from any educational provider, and its education-specific function, also lends weight to the likelihood that the institution will fall into line. Yet compliance in the UK is not guaranteed with the same reliability as in New Zealand, given the non-compulsory nature of the OIA's resolutions.

Regulation and student wellbeing: fieldwork findings

Formal regulation reveals gaps in student welfare, some of which are addressed in the public debate reviewed above, but some of which are not on the agenda in either the debate or the foreseeable policies of government. Regulation theory suggests that this renders self-regulation and the informal sphere more generally of greater importance than they otherwise would be. As not only theory but also data from student and policy and service-level staff made clear, however, the picture is more complex than a rudimentary replacement of informal for formal. Information on and for regulation is a vital ingredient.

Students are only partially aware of the rules to which they are subject in most areas. Some seek to make up for the shortfall in information by not suffering diminutions in their perceived life opportunities and generally having positive experiences of overseas education. Often they make up for formal shortfalls through informal channels incorporating trans-national and local family, friendship and representative community organisation networks. No formula offers full life satisfaction. Many students do not have what they deem a satisfactory range of network options.

Staff interviewee perceptions add necessary complexity to the picture. As well as information problems, the data revealed varying levels of awareness among policy personnel and university staff informants of whether the ESOS Framework may be welfare-adequate. Service-level staff demonstrated greater recognition, although they were generally in organisationally less privileged positions than their policy-level contemporaries and thus less able to address formal regulatory problems to effect enhancements. In both staff and student data, a key theme lies in the conceptual differences between pastoral care, consumer protection for market maintenance, and welfare, and the notion that students may be deserving of protections that are either not inherent within the ESOS Framework or not currently effectively enforceable. Such a perspective allows the analyst – and more importantly, the policy maker and formal regulator – to imagine a more generous and necessarily trans-national kind of student citizenship than the mainly economic variety which is available to international students in Australia under contemporary arrangements.

Regulatory information availability

Despite significant efforts by providers to furnish students with as much relevant information on regulation as possible, students in general did not demonstrate high levels of awareness of the rules which partially govern their overseas welfare experience. The most quoted *sources* of information, for example, were not local Australian officials or provider representatives, but pre-departure information at exhibitions and expos, agents and representatives from Australian international education marketing and service organisation, IDP. Websites were also a prominent source. A fuller picture is provided in Table 5.1, while noting that some students mentioned more than one source of information.

Table 5.1: Most quoted sources of information about Australian education and studying abroad, among those who cited their sources

	Number	%
Friends/relative in Australia	48	24
Education exhibition/agent/IDP/ in home country	79	40
Website/internet	61	31
Australian embassy/High Commission	3	1.5
Friends/colleagues in home country	3	1.5
Newspaper in home country	2	1.

Note: Total number of international students = 200.

More generally, of the 200 student interviewees, 146 reported having at least some prior knowledge about the Australian education system, while 54 stated that they had little or 'not much' knowledge.

Student perceptions of their welfare

Shortfalls in regulatory information and low cognisance and recognition of regulations can result in students not realising the nature and extent of protections that the ESOS Framework and other laws in existence provide. This, as Chapter Six discusses at length, is a similar problem in the case of New Zealand. Logically and in practice this information deficit results in students not *accessing* services. For some there was a perception that more needed to be done formally. When asked a general question, 'Should better back-up systems be provided to students while they are in Australia?', 143 answered 'yes', while 30 said 'no' and 27 reported that either they were not sure or provided no answer. The resulting shortfalls in support, perceived and substantive, are interrogated at length in Marginson et al (2010).

Some seek to substitute what they perceive to be gaps in formal rules with informal welfare sources. As revealed in Table 5.2 below, of students who reported feeling some level of loneliness at stages of their time in the host country (131), friendships were prioritised for needed support within the host country, and family and relatives in the home country.

Table 5.2: Emotional support for students reporting loneliness (n = 131)

	Source of emotional support
Relationships in Australia	
Family/relatives	15
Friends	71
University staff	11
Relationships in home country	
Family/relatives	45
Friends	12

Note: Some students use more than one source.

Family also predominated in financial support, with 123 students stating that this was the top source in times of trouble with or elementary need of money. For broader social support 96 reported involvement in community or social organisations. Thus slightly more than half of the students, 104, had either no involvement in such organisations or did not report any.

Policy and service-level staff perceptions

The perceptions of staff at the level of both policy and service provision are important. Staff play the more central role in regulation and its implementation than students, who rely mostly on self-regulation and informal sources. The greater regulatory detail provided in the staff interviews justifies less numerical and more qualitative appraisal.

Importantly, some policy staff reported a generalised faith in the ESOS Framework as a source of welfare for students (Oz 1, 3). They shared this with certain service staff (Oz 7, 9). Others viewed particular *aspects* of ESOS favourably, such as its dealings with consumer protection (Oz 1), immigration (Oz 5) and the relationship between the immigration and education ministries (Oz 5, 9). Others saw it as positive for other reasons including as a means of regulating the 'industry' (Oz 2), as a legal path creating greater public and policy awareness of international students and the issues they face (Oz 2), and as a mechanism for protecting students against the unethical behaviour of some providers (Oz 4, 9).

The most significant point, however, is that interviewees generally had narrower views than those that exist in some scholarly literature on what constitutes welfare, largely relegating issues beyond consumer protection (and to a lesser extent pastoral care) to realms other than international education. While all interviewees agreed that New South Wales and Victoria should allow international students the same access to public transport concessions as students in other states and local students in all states, two policy informants were particularly forthcoming in their opposition to any form of direct income support or subsidy other than scholarships such as those from AusAID (Australian Government Overseas Aid Programme) (Oz, 3, 4). One of these interviewees based their opposition on fiscal grounds:

> 'I can't see it [income support] as being practical actually; that is one of the things. I mean, this is such a large industry that the fiscal impact of that would just not be accepted by government or by the public either, I don't think.' (Oz 3)

The other interviewee was stronger in denouncing income support in any form other than targeted scholarships:

> 'I think [income support] it's completely inappropriate.... I can't see the policy justification for income support for international students, to be honest. I can see, for example,

during the Asian economic crisis, throughout the industry there were a lot of kids [international students] who were suddenly stranded because the family factory [in the home country] went broke. And there was a lot of negotiation with embassies in country, but with universities who did all sorts of things to enable them to pay fees in instalments and delayed payments, or complete the semester before they had to leave. But to go any further than that would be just making a burden on the Australian taxpayer.' (Oz 4)

The opposition of this informant came not only from the fiscal point of view, nominating the additional international relations criterion of 'buying influence' from developing countries, hence essentially viewing support as education-related aid for the purpose of improving Australia's position vis-à-vis Asia.

'If the government is going to provide income support, then how about we look at where we think, depending on what your philosophy behind it is, are we buying influence, in which case we do this [take certain approach]. Is it altruistically motivated in its aid, in which we do this [an alternate approach]? Are we worried about an arc of [political] instability, in which case we go for a few police checks [on students].' (Oz 4)

The informant is alluding to the nationally instituted but internationally oriented foreign policy character of potential income support measures, which she deems "completely inappropriate". The student is constructed in market, full-fee terms, with the best of protections offered being simple, temporary fee relief to compensate for the market failure that was the Asian financial crisis of the late 1990s. Far from entertaining social and economic policies that would effectively constitute subsidies in healthcare and accommodation costs, for example, the most prominent view among staff interviewees, of the purpose of ESOS, was as a framework for providing consumer protection (Oz 1, 3, 4, 7). As one termed it, the purpose was "consumer protection for prospective students who have to buy before they try" (Oz 4). The same interviewee expanded slightly by stating that ESOS was about "making providers responsible for what their agents do and say" (Oz 4). For some of these informants consumer protection was a means to maintaining market share, one praising the legislation and National Code on the grounds that "[i]t [ESOS] is a very good thing to have for the protection of students and protection of reputation of Australian education as well" (Oz 3). For others ESOS was essentially a combination of consumer protection and quality assurance:

'It is in essence a piece of, it has two fundamental purposes: consumer protection for prospective students … and part of what I call, I call it one of the pillars of the Australian quality framework, that's my small "a", small "q", small "f" underpinning international education.' (Oz 7)

Staff at service level – and surprisingly, policy staff as well – displayed low levels of knowledge of alternatives to ESOS, and the concept of pastoral care was not prominent in interview interpretations of its purpose. Rather, when mentioned, pastoral care was discussed in the context of the weaknesses of the framework (Oz 4, 5, 9, 12). One informant summed it up: "I think it [ESOS] should articulate what the goals *are* as far as pastoral care and support of students and I think that providers should then be the ones that decide how that is going to be achieved" (Oz 9).

Perceptions of alternative regulatory frameworks to ESOS were few, casting doubt as to the validity, in higher education regulators' minds, of the need for a comparative perspective for the purposes of reform. When asked about whether Australia needed an independent regulator in the form of an external adjudicator such as New Zealand's IEAA, those responses that were unequivocal were mixed, with some saying 'yes' (Oz 9, 13) and some saying 'no' (Oz 1, 2). Interestingly, the 'yes' response came exclusively from service providers while the 'no' emanated only from policy staff. Thus only the service providers, who are closer to the needs of students – because they saw needs through their service provision at the front line – saw potential utility in an independent adjudicator. The policy staff, who by definition have a greater capacity to effect regulatory change than service providers, were unanimous in opposing it.

When asked about the formal framework in Australia's nearest neighbour and one of its major competitors in international education, New Zealand, with its Pastoral Care Code, it was clear by means of the absence of substantive knowledge that the informants did not generally see such an approach as a realistic one for Australia. This is regardless of any personal or unofficial preferences they may have had. One policy informant did not know of the New Zealand Code at all (Oz 3).

On the question of coordination between areas of regulation relevant to student welfare, some thought that the nexus between education and migration was either not well conceived or not clear to students and thus in need of reform (Oz 2, 5, 7, 8, 10, 12, 13). Others focused their feedback regarding coordination on providers and information on academic progress (Oz 7) and university disciplinary issues (Oz 8), while another group saw the problem lying in differences between states in the implementation of ESOS guidelines (Oz 2, 3, 4). As discussed in Chapters Seven and Eight later, the comparative and global analyses, this is significant for regulation, given that a great deal of evidence exists regarding the benefits of 'whole-of-government', consultative and similar approaches.

Finally, there is the implicit need for greater student reliance on informal welfare than would normally be the case, suggested not only by student data as discussed above, but also by staff perceptions. The clearest instances of this need were in relation to students' 'social isolation' and associated problems of 'loneliness' and 'culture shock', with most staff interviewees identifying these as significant (Oz 2, 4, 7, 8, 9, 12, 13). Another added that the most important issue relating to student feelings of isolation was pressure from family, and especially parents, from the home country (Oz 13).

Conclusion

The Australian model is one characterised by a great deal of formal regulatory codification, much of which is law. Some of the law conforms with the traditional model of command-and-control public administration, or what lawyers refer to as 'black letter'. Yet much of this formalisation applies only to compliance by educational institutions. Those factors that affect student wellbeing are typically those which are dressed up as student protections but are in practice either not enforceable or subject to the final prerogative of the education provider rather than the student. Independent regulation is sparse and provisions for it are so new as to be largely untried. The situation is only exacerbated by the lack of knowledge of the protections that do exist on the part of students, but perhaps most surprisingly, also staff, and more surprisingly still, policy staff more than service staff.

This is a picture of a regime with a student welfare deficit. Given that the emphasis in the ESOS Framework – reinforced by strong and clear staff interviewee perceptions – is on consumer protection, the central conclusion to be drawn is that the formal regulatory programme of Australia is one which pursues global market share over and above genuine concerns for student wellbeing.

—

As revealed in the next chapter and the one following, in this there are some compelling similarities with New Zealand. These similarities are surprising, given the emphasis in New Zealand's formal rules on 'pastoral care' rather than consumer protection.

Notes

[1] Unless otherwise stated, references here made purely to 'Sections' are to Jackson and Varnham's (2007) *Law for educators*. As noted this is the only major up-to-date and comprehensive legal text covering the area.

SIX

Pastoral care, minimal information: the New Zealand model

Introduction

Similar to Australia, the New Zealand model of international education regulation has a great many formal provisions when viewed alongside other common law countries. New Zealand is a signatory to GATS. There are similar regulations on migration through international education, although these are currently less strict than their Australian counterparts. There are rules governing the provision of TNHE and quality assurance. Although New Zealand has individual legal provisions, these are also less elaborate than those of Australia in their implementation, due mainly to the unitary rather than federal nature of the New Zealand constitution; hence there is no need for federal–regional liaison in the formulation and implementation of law.

Assessed in terms of how its regime constructs and addresses student welfare, New Zealand stands apart from its neighbour in having a *Code of practice for the pastoral care of international students* (the Pastoral Care Code or simply, the Code). This has many similarities to Australia's ESOS Framework, but also key differences that form the main focus of this chapter. Further, covered under the same code in New Zealand is the now almost decade-long existence of a student grievance body, compulsorily ruling over welfare-related issues that are not solved to the parties' satisfaction after a student complaint is lodged – the IEAA, or the Appeal Authority.

The objective of this chapter is to analyse the New Zealand regulation regime, using existing literature and primary data from both enrolled international students and service and policy-level staff informants. The interview data are analogous to those used for Australia, although as described in Chapter One, these are proportionate and appropriate to the smaller size of the population and the nation's education sector, relying accordingly on fewer universities, a smaller number of students and a slightly lower number of staff interviewees. The rationales behind the student and staff data are the same as they are for Australia, namely, to cover student self-perceptions of welfare and related services, staff feedback to supplement student data but also central to uncovering the rationales behind, the gaps in, and the strengths of, the formal national regulation sphere. Insights into the *in*formal sphere are necessarily also explored.

The mix of formal and informal, as derived from the interview data, is key to the central finding of the chapter. In New Zealand, so is the trade-based – perhaps trade-*biased* – nature of the Pastoral Care Code, which renders the New Zealand regime more fundamentally similar to Australia than a mere examination of the formal regulations alone might reveal. Further to the same point, but worthy of separate mention, is the near absence of knowledge among students of the Pastoral Care Code in general and the Appeal Authority in particular. In short, it is as if the regulatory authorities forgot to tell most international students of the merits of the regime's explicit pastoral care focus, despite the benefits for both parties, in relation to trade and student welfare respectively. This finding, along with the deficiencies of New Zealand's pastoral care model as a welfare tool, serves as an ongoing challenge for that country's policy makers and legislators.

In support of its central finding the chapter begins by outlining the legal context of international student welfare in New Zealand, discussing the individual national legal provisions governing higher education. The second section overviews the Pastoral Care Code, with an emphasis on its welfare provisions. The third section explores the continuing debate on the regulatory contours of student welfare in New Zealand. Principally through student and staff interview data analysis, the fourth and largest section analyses the role of the informal welfare sphere. The fifth and final section draws together the broader regulatory implications of the New Zealand model.

Higher education law context: individual legal provisions

Unlike the situation for the US, the UK and Australia, there is no comprehensive text outlining in an authoritative way the higher education law framework in New Zealand. The area requires piecing together from a wider range of sources.

Similarly to their Australian counterparts, New Zealand's universities were established under legislation. With a unitary state and a smaller population, however, a single Act of Parliament incorporating all of them was used. The New Zealand University Act of 1870 established the nation's first institution, the University of Otago, but all universities established thereafter became part of the federated University of New Zealand, beginning with the University of Auckland (Archives New Zealand, 2011). The situation changed in 1961 with the disestablishment of the Act. Universities could thereafter take independent identities and grant their own qualifications.

Universities are themselves simultaneously subject to many Acts of Parliament, reflecting a similar range of issues regulated as noted previously for the US, the UK and Australia. When viewed closely the number of Acts that apply on university campuses and in relation to university affairs is surprisingly large. Victoria University of Wellington (VUW), for example, notes that it is subject to at least 62 separate legislative instruments, legislative amendments and accompanying regulations (VUW, 2011). This is not an exhaustive list. Apart from the 1961 legislation establishing its formal independence from the University of New Zealand and the New Zealand University Act, contemporary issues covered under law for VUW include but are not limited to: the education product itself (Education Act 1989 and various amending laws); buildings (Building Act 2004); defamation issues (Defamation Act 1992); and equal pay for equal work and employment conditions more widely conceived (Equal Pay Act 1972 and Employment Relations Act 2000).

In practice the list is a great deal longer. For the tertiary sector as a whole, students' rights as consumers of a commercial product are covered under the Consumer Guarantees Act 1973 and the Fair Trading Act 1986. These rights are constructed by the Acts in terms of the student–institution contractual or pseudo-contractual relationship. Academic freedoms are governed mainly under Section 161(2) of the Education Act. Section 160 of the same Act recognises the 'accountability' that academic institutions must show to their students in the face of the academic freedoms enshrined in Section 161. The Education Amendment Act 1990 had as one of its main objectives the administration of institutions, including the recognition of qualifications in tertiary and vocational education and the promotion of excellence in education and research (Lim and Hyatt, 2009, pp 23-8).

Students' rights as legal citizens are covered, inter alia, under the Privacy Act 1993, the Human Rights Act 1993, the New Zealand Bill of Rights Act 1990 and the Ombudsmen Act 1975. Under the Official Information Act 1982 students can also officially request reasons for their grades (Lim and Hyatt, 2009, p 29). In addition, students have rights under the quality assurance framework, incorporating the New Zealand Qualifications Authority (NZQA) for vocational colleges, and for the universities the Committee on University Academic Programmes (CUAP) of the New Zealand Vice Chancellors Committee (NZVCC) (ENZ, 2005, pp 14-15). The Tertiary Education Commission (TEC) funds the government's contribution to tertiary education and training (NZQA, 2011). Students can act on their rights in relation to their withdrawals from courses, and refunds. Their fees are also protected in the event of institution insolvency or institution deregistration by the NZQA. Finally, NZQA provides an avenue for student complaints in relation to quality issues.

International students' rights are subject to a specific body of regulations encapsulated in the Code of Practice for the Pastoral Care of International Students 2002 (MOENZ, 2010).

Pastoral Care Code

International education in New Zealand is relatively independent and arguably less complex than that of Australia. The federal structure of the Australian Constitution and the ESOS Framework's more indirect and compliance-focused language renders the New Zealand code more focused.

A major point of difference between Australia and New Zealand stems from the fact that the latter has a nationally applicable, independent student complaints and appeals body. This was established under the Pastoral Care Code and is called the International Education Appeal Authority. Similarly to the Australian situation, the New Zealand Code is part of a broader framework of quality assurance, consumer protection and pastoral care, although its pastoral care provisions are significantly more specific and far-reaching. Given the more recent emergence of international education as a high-ranking export industry for the national economy of New Zealand (MOENZ, 2006), international students were noteworthy for their 'absence' in public regulation before the introduction of the Pastoral Care Code (Butcher, 2003).

The Pastoral Care Code, which operates alongside quality mechanisms, is designed to ensure that providers offer fair treatment and pastoral care to international students studying onshore in New Zealand. Although Australia's ESOS Framework has legal rules and generalised guidelines on 'welfare services' for students, there is no framework in that country which institutionalises pastoral care in the manner of the New Zealand Code. Similarly to the ESOS Framework, however, New Zealand's programme enshrines regulations regarding course and university marketing (Part 2, Sections 4 and 5, or Parts 2.4-2.5), student recruitment (Parts 2.6-2.2.7) and enrolment (Parts 2.9-

2.10). Under Part 2 (Section 4), information provided to prospective students must include: 'costs of tuition and other course-related costs', application requirements, conditions of acceptance, refund conditions, English language proficiency requirements, facilities, equipment and staffing, courses or qualifications offered by the provider, medical and travel insurance requirements, and types of accommodation applicable to students (Part 2.4). As well as requirements for providers, the Code incorporates rules governing relations between providers and their student recruitment agents (Part 3.11) and accommodation agents (Part 3.11). In addition both kinds of agent must be provided with or led to a copy of the Code and must operate within its guidelines.

On the formal regulation of student rights, however, the New Zealand Code is distinguished by two dimensions: first, the breadth and specificity of its provisions on welfare (Part 5) and accommodation (Part 6); and second, the strength of its grievance procedures (Part 7). On the first of these, providers must have a designated internal staff member or unit that deals explicitly with pastoral care for cross-border students, and the existence of this person or unit 'must be advised to students on enrolment' (Part 15.1). Providers must also offer 'support services' including: an appropriate orientation programme (Part 15.2.1); assistance to students facing problems with cultural adaptation (Part 15.2.2); and 'advocacy procedures, to ensure that students are aware of their rights and the signatory's [provider's] obligations under the Code and how to access internal and external grievance procedures.' Also under support services, providers must furnish students with: information and advice on accommodation, 'including advice on whether the signatory has assessed the suitability of any accommodation and the result of any such assessment' (Part 15.3.1); information on driving laws and safety on the roads (Part 15.3.2) and other laws including the sale of tobacco and alcohol (Part 15.3.6); advice on welfare facilities, including personal health services, mental health services, drug education and counselling, and problem gambling (Part 15.3.4); information on sexual education and reproductive health services, health promotion (Part 15.3.5); and information and advice on harassment and discrimination (Part 15.3.7). These are all matters on which Australian law is less articulate, although protections for students under 18 are similar in the two countries (Parts 15-7-15.12).

Provision for grievance procedures in New Zealand, on all issues covered in the Pastoral Care Code, encompasses internal procedures (Part 7.24) that are similar to Australian rules under the ESOS Act, although the wording of the New Zealand Code makes markedly more explicit the obligations of providers (Part 7.24). The most pivotal difference, however, lies in the existence of New Zealand's Appeal Authority, established under Part 7, Section 25 of the Code. Once cross-border students consider that they have a problem that the Code may address, but have exhausted the internal avenues of the provider to address it, students can seek redress from the IEAA (Part 7.25.5). The IEAA hears the case, seeks appropriate information from all interests and makes its decision, which is binding on all parties (Part 7.26). A range of penalties can apply (Parts 7.26.2-7.26.5) and the matter can be elevated to the International Education Review Panel if unresolved (Parts 27 and 28), a body that has higher and ultimate authority on legal matters stemming from and relating to the Code. Also, the IEAA must report to an administrator of the Code in summary form every three months and to the public with case notes and data summary annually (Part 7.25.4). This is attractive with respect to transparency, a universal requirement to responsive regulation. It is noteworthy that the Review Panel has rarely been activated, a factor discussed in the analysis of interview data in the fourth section of this chapter.

Regulatory debate

As shown in the last chapter, Australia's international education debate has centred on whether the regime is too commercialised and thus focused on the international student fee dollar; provider quality and financial viability concerns and associated questions of pathways to education-based skilled migration; exchange rate and market share issues; the cultural and social benefits of international education; welfare and safety and crime concerns; and the potential merits of an education ombudsman or similar independent body to hear and process student grievances in the case of a stalemate between student and institution.

Public debate in New Zealand displays similar characteristics, and also some differences. The Australian issues led directly to several major government and parliamentary inquiries and taskforces, with the major result being changes to the international student migration dimension. Other than temporary falls in market share, stemming from diplomatic issues between the New Zealand and Chinese governments in the mid-2000s amid issues of racism against Chinese and Asian students (see Chapter Four), the New Zealand debate has been more settled and less controversial.

Student grievance regime

New Zealand has had the IEAA since the inception of the Pastoral Care Code in 2002 under Section 238F of the Education Act 1989. Covering both the VET and higher education sectors, and indeed also schools, New Zealand's Code specifies a central role in both the care of students and the nation's international competitive positioning for independent grievance handling through the IEAA. Under Part 7 of the Code, where internal grievance procedures do not resolve a complaint to the satisfaction of the student, the IEAA exists to 'receive and adjudicate on complaints received from international students and their authorised agents/representatives, or by the Administrator, concerning alleged breaches of the Code' (Section 25.1), where the administrator refers to 'the person or organisation responsible for the administration of the Code'. IEAA decisions are binding on both education institution and student and/or may be referred to a different legal tribunal or court.

Alternatively, unresolved matters may remain within the ambit of the Code but referred above the IEAA to the International Education Review Panel (Section 27; MOENZ, 2011a, Section 25). In sum, in formal code, contrary to Australia, New Zealand provides a substantial voice to students through national, independent, international education-focused grievance handling.

The Code

There are challenges relating to how the IEAA provisions translate – and in some dimensions do not – into welfare on the ground for students. A review of the Code was undertaken in 2010 but changes made as a result were mainly limited to school education, and in particular relating to approval processes by the Code administrator, accommodation for students under 18 years of age and the offer of a place and enrolment procedures. In addition a relatively minor change in migration on the skilled category has been enacted which has extended the allowable graduate work search period to two years (MOENZ, 2011a). Save for the recommendations of some service providers that students need greater external advocacy and support before the IEAA, the overriding perception of interviewees is that the IEAA is relatively effective in meeting its objectives. However, this needs to be placed in context, principally by reference to the fieldwork findings.

Regulation and student wellbeing: fieldwork findings

On the one hand, New Zealand interview data collected from students and policy and service personnel reveals a general if often qualified sense of confidence in the Pastoral Care Code's effectiveness. This is certainly a stronger confidence than Australian interviewees had in their ESOS Framework. But digging deeper into the New Zealand data shows evidence of gaps in the provision of welfare and in welfare regulation, and inconsistencies in views between staff and students.

Unearthing a bigger and more detailed canvass involves not only unpacking general perceptions of the Code and its effectiveness as a tool for providing or enhancing student welfare; it also entails examining views of the role and effectiveness of the IEAA as a provider or fixer of last resort. The mix between formal and informal welfare sources is also relevant, as are questions of trade and commercialism against concepts of welfare, pastoral care and consumer protection.

Perceptions of the Code and its effectiveness

New Zealand staff interviewees were overridingly less equivocal than their Australian counterparts in approving of the Code under which they operate (see especially NZ 1, 2, 3, 4, 5, 7, 9, 11).[1]

> 'I think the Code provides us with a really good ... I think it's been really good.' (NZ 7)
> 'I think it's got the formula right.' (NZ 4)
> 'My personal view is I think it's about right.' (NZ 9)
> 'My gut feeling is [the Code] it's pretty right. I think in general it has been very well accepted by the sector.' (NZ 2)
> 'The general impression [among stakeholders] seems to be that the Code is good. The Code administrator's office does their job well. The other structures in place are effective.' (NZ 2)
> 'Generally the response from people on the ground level is the Code is fantastic.' (NZ 8)

Approval was generally stronger among policy staff than among service staff (NZ 6, 8, 10), who arguably tend to be best qualified to judge since they are closer to the ground level, at the shop floor, where student issues are raised and dealt with in direct fashion. Yet qualifications to overarching approval from even policy staff were more specific in some instances. When asked about the general effectiveness of the Code, NZ 1, for example, reflected:

'I think primarily I would like to see better compliance. And so that's about the systems [of, or introduced by, the Code], improving that. And improving the Code, I think for me at the moment, [the need] is improving the way the Code is policed by the International Education Appeal Authority, and promoted and monitored.'

Others agreed, particularly on compliance, adding questions of the Code administrator's role:

'[W]e ought to be looking at the administrator's office, and what resources they have available; and how they're able to do that monitoring and semi-enforcement role, rather than the information provision and Code signatory role.' (NZ 2)

This interviewee was manifestly not alone in this:

'I think you have a problem where you have one sanction at the end and nothing sort of in between. In most enforcement and compliance regimes there is a variety of sanctions between say prosecution and providing information.' (NZ 3)

Similar questions were raised by staff over other aspects of the Code. This includes: the role and power of agents that the Code allows (NZ 4); various student welfare issues and notably its lack of attention to mental health (NZ 10, 11); and the relationship between the Code office and institutions (NZ 8).

Who knows, and who knows what, about the Code?

Staff assessments of the Code are not balanced unless viewed alongside student interviewees' perceptions. After all, all staff interviewees work with the Code in one way or another. Most argued that naturally students knew about the Code (see especially NZ 1, 2, 3, 4, 5, 8, 10, 11). One senior academic and administrative university figure was particularly emphatic when asked if students were aware of the Code: "Oh yes, international students arc. We've got it on our website. We promote it. We want them to be aware of it" (NZ 5). Another was a little more concerned, implicitly arguing that too many students had no awareness:"The only time they [international students] really know about the Code is when something [negative] happens" (NZ 4).

The challenge in exploring *student* views, on the other hand, was that they had little or no knowledge of it. The majority of students, 63 per cent, were not aware that in New Zealand there existed a Code that sought to provide for the pastoral care of international students. Sixty-one per cent did not know that universities were bound by a Code. The students who did know of the Code even included a few who were employed part time in the university, in jobs such as research assistant and library assistant. As one student reflected:

> 'Yes I know about that [the Code] because it is part of my job. If I am not working there I may not know this.' (S 19)
> Some others had knowledge of the Code because of problems with rules relating to fees, which prompted a student rally:
> 'No, first time I heard of that code. I sort of knew because I have problems with fee because the university tried to change the fee payment method which was we were paying in US$, and last year they tried to changed to NZ$ but the currency wasn't quite alright because they were tried to use in the peak currency but compared to what the currency at the time was we could pay far less than what they were asking us to pay so a lot of people like gather together and speak to the deputy of university. Then at that time after that because they listened to us then we now we pay US$ which we wanted to and it was so amazing to see that school actually listened to the students yes it was quite helpful.' (S 34)

Students were also asked a more specific question regarding what aspects of student pastoral care were included in the Code. Eighty-four per cent said they did not know what aspects specifically the Code covered. Some students could only make a guess:

> '[G]enerally that's a lot of things I think but what I know is that the universities have the obligation to look after international students in terms of academic [that is, related to classroom and study] if for example I don't understanding anything relating to university works and I present the problem to someone and they have to help me.' (S 42)

Others had varying ideas regarding coverage: "I think it just means you need to provide healthcare, you need to provide maybe a person that we can talk to as well" (S 4); "I only know that they must provide the certain health for international students" (S 23); "Yeh insurance policy and everything?" (S 27); "International student welfare, health, safety, educational needs, I don't think they do financially for you" (S 45); "Yes they like payment of fees and everyday premise such qualification then they must provide that amount of papers and hours" (S 57); "Security probably and accommodation for students? I don't know" (S 63).

Confirming other studies (Sawir et al, 2009a, 2009b), language difficulties pose a significant issue for international students in New Zealand. Interviews for this book revealed that almost half of the students had language difficulties (46 per cent). Problems with English language constituted a barrier for international students in seeking to understand the Code. Feedback from the following students substantiates the point:

> 'Yes [I know about the Code], but I didn't read through because it's like things really complicated, I didn't read through the thing.' (S 63)

> 'Well I guess I can try to find out to know about [provisions of the Code] but I am not someone who likes to read legal stuff, and they have really very difficult English. I don't know what it actually consists of.' (S 1)

Table 6.1 provides a summary of the feedback offered by the 70 students in relation to their knowledge of Code content.

Table 6.1: Summary of students' understanding of the content of the Code

	Question	Yes	%	No	%	Not sure	%
a.	Did you know universities and agents must provide you with complete information on all course-related costs before you sign anything?	40	57	30	43	–	–
	Was this done?	62	88	4	6	4	6
b.	Did you know university promotional material must provide 'a fair and accurate representation' of the services offered to you by the university?	39	56	31	44	–	–
	Was this done?	52	74	6	9	12	17
c.	Did you know you must be provided with accurate information on the cost and availability of accommodation, before you sign anything?	40	57	30	43	–	–
	Was this done?	56	80	3	4	11	16
d.	Did you know that the university must provide 'assistance to students facing difficulty in adapting to the new cultural environment'?	36	51	34	49	–	–
	Was this provided?	54	77	6	9	10	14
e.	Did you know that the university must provide 'information and advice in relation to accommodation', and must provide a person to assist you with accommodation problems?	30	43	40	57	–	–
	Was this provided?	45	64	14	20	11	16
f.	Did you know that the university must provide 'information and advice in relation to welfare facilities, including personal health services, mental health services, drug education and counselling, and problem gambling'?	40	57	30	43	–	–
	Was this provided?	56	80	7	10	7	10
g.	Also 'information and advice on accessing information on sexuality education, health promotion, and sexual and reproductive health services'?	39	56	27	39	4	6
	Was this provided?	51	73	7	10	12	17
h.	Did you know that the university must provide 'information and advice on addressing harassment and discrimination'?	41	73	29	41	–	–
	Was this provided?	55	79	6	9	9	13
i.	Did you know that if the university believes you are unable to protect yourself from harm or unable to safeguard your own welfare, the university is obliged to monitor your living conditions, and meet regularly with you to make sure you are okay?	11	16	59	84	–	–
	Is this done in such cases, to your knowledge?	15	21	24	34	31	44
j.	Did you know that if you are in this situation, the university 'must communicate regularly with appropriate persons' including, if necessary, your parents or next of kin?	18	26	52	74	–	–

The IEAA

Some staff interviewees viewed the IEAA in generally positive terms, even if it was mainly because they saw in it an important body with the function of providing an independent regulatory voice (NZ 1, 7, 8, 9, 11). One interviewee summed this up by saying:

> 'I think it is important that it [the IEAA] exists and its role is like an ombudsman. And I think that international students have to be aware that the Appeal Authority does exist for them.' (NZ 11)

While also generally acknowledging the importance of its function, others saw its existence as a challenge to institutional autonomy, with some bemoaning the associated compliance burden (NZ 1, 7, 8), although this was rarely explicitly stated. For example, one interviewee summed up by arguing: "[T]he only complaints that are taken to the IEAA are against education providers, rather than 'accommodation agent [and] recruitment agents'." Another reflected: "Most of the IEAA's decisions tend to be in favour of the student" (NZ 7).

Staff perceptions of the *importance* of the IEAA varied directly with views on whether it was a potential threat to the autonomy of education institutions. This was stated clearly by an interviewee at the policy level with wide experience in various parts of the New Zealand educational bureaucracy:

> 'There are split views within the [broader international education] industry on the Appeal Authority, and you [the interviewer] probably would have heard them. You're going around talking to a lot of universities. Universities are a bit more lukewarm on the Appeal Authority, simply because they have their own internal processes and appeals and all that sort of stuff.' (NZ 9)

One staff interviewee argued that students only truly "know about" the Code when "something [negative] happens" (NZ 4, quoted above). This interviewee could also have been reflecting more specifically on the IEAA, which technically applies specifically to Section 7 of the Code. And many student interviewees would concur, particularly so because knowledge of the IEAA was particularly scarce. Students were asked if they knew that New Zealand had an authority that they could appeal to if a complaint to the education provider was not dealt with to the student's satisfaction. Ninety per cent said 'no'. Some thought that this was something that their agent should know about and should advise them on: "No, but I think my agent would know about that" (S 41). Some expressed scepticism in relation to the potential usefulness of the IEAA (for example, S 19, 21, 15).

For reasons that were not explored in the student interviews, few students stated that they needed or wanted more or better information from their institution on the IEAA. One who did, however, made it abundantly clear:

> '[W]hat I think the Code of Practice could do. One of thing is let us know the rules of whole things so we can know what you should do to me or something like if you don't say we just don't know, and we don't know what rights we have, what benefit they should [offer us].' (S 15)

The clearest message emerging from the combined discussion of staff and student interview data, therefore, was that the effectiveness of formal regulation was seriously curtailed by a deficit in knowledge of and about the central instruments of regulation: the Code and the IEAA.

Informal sphere

Given this poor state of knowledge, do students regulate their own lives by less formal means, any more than would in ordinary circumstances be the case, that is, in their home country? As discussed earlier, staff expressed a generalised or qualified faith in the Pastoral Care Code's effectiveness in delivering on its promise of student care. However, that is not the end of the story, because even if only by logic the existence of the formal sphere presupposes an *in*formal sphere. This, in turn, brings to light the welfare issues that students face in practice. In relation to Australia these were discussed at book length in Marginson et al (2010). For New Zealand a similar account is presented by Sawir et al (2009a, 2009b), with some differences, but using student data, with an overriding suggestion that in New Zealand students face similar gaps in their welfare under the Code as their counterparts in Australia under the ESOS Framework.

Service-providing staff in New Zealand, who as part of their daily work see the issues faced by students, pointed to gaps in the formal regulation of welfare (see especially NZ 10, 11), which are partially filled by, and naturally call forth, greater priority in informal mechanisms. This was substantiated in student feedback. Thirty-six per cent of students reported financial difficulties at some stage of their time in New Zealand. Of those students who had engaged in part-time or casual employment, 47 per cent had experienced problems at work. A small proportion of those, 9 per cent, reported that they had received pay or conditions less than those of New Zealand employees who would be, or were, doing the same or similar work. Forty-six per cent said that the English language created problems for them in their academic work, and a minority regarded the International English Language Testing System (IELTS) test that they had undergone before acceptance into studies was inadequate preparation (for example, S 35, 46, 54, 59).

Forty-three per cent reported having experienced discrimination, most of which was off campus, with language difficulties prompting racist or otherwise discriminatory behaviour on the part of perpetrators (for example, S 5, 8, 13, 14, 64, 66, 69). Thirty-nine per cent had had health problems while in New Zealand. On questions of safety, 90 per cent reported feeling safe, with the remaining 10 per cent reflecting on experiences of lack of safety, mainly due to drunken behaviour on the part of perpetrators, although a few had experienced being robbed (for example, S 53, 64).

The more central question in the current analysis, however, is that of social isolation, which more than any other indicator prompts the need for informal welfare. Students seek out informal networks regardless of the character of the formal welfare regime, but loneliness makes informal support all the more necessary. Students were asked the question: 'Have you experienced periods of loneliness or isolation?' In response several remarked that the overseas experience was exciting because it gave them space for more self-determination and independence. Others described the experience as a long and lonely journey, and 66 per cent had experienced at least one significant period of loneliness or isolation in their time in New Zealand. This did not mean they were *constantly* lonely. Feelings of loneliness were most likely in the initial period of stay.

> 'When you first came to a new place…. There was the usual accommodation offered by the university. Most of my friends got to stay in the university hall. I applied but I didn't get in. If you stay in the university hall at least you still get to meet people who have come [to New Zealand] with you. From what I heard from others it's easier to make friends. But for me, once I came here I started to look for a flat on my own and I stayed outside university. You don't get to meet people. You have this kind of homesickness.

> You don't know how to relate to people because most of the time you meet Kiwis with their accents and you don't understand them.' (Female, S23, Psychology, Malaysia)

In addition, research students could be lonely due to the solitary nature of their everyday (mainly thesis-based) work. They lacked a classroom because of the individuality of the research process. In a class, students could at least meet contemporaries and make friends.

> 'You are [one is] very frustrated, because you are here alone. It's full of expectations when you come overseas. Even though there is no pressure from anyone you tend to drive yourself very hard because you self-support yourself here, and so expect a high level of academic achievement from yourself. The work piles up and sometimes you just don't feel like doing it, but you have to meet the deadline. That's when you get really depressed and you are frustrated and you don't really know why.' (Female, S28, Geography, Singapore)

When asked how they coped when they felt lonely, the majority of students mentioned links with close friends in the host country, and calling parents, relatives and friends in the home country. Other students went online, watched movies, listened to music and went out with friends. Some just retreated into themselves. As the same student above reflected, "Well, sometimes I don't really like talking to anyone."

Beyond trade? Consumer protection, pastoral care and welfare

A significant proportion of the student data thus reveals gaps in welfare that were similar to those reported by international students in Australia. Accordingly students in New Zealand, like their counterparts across the Tasman Sea, showed a high reliance on informal welfare, and some service-providing staff pointed in their responses to issues that were consistent with gaps in formal regulation, given the kinds of problems they were presented with on a regular basis.

The question of the basis of the New Zealand regulatory regime is raised. It is revealed in this chapter that it does not provide pastoral care, even using the cumulative conception of these words in the official Pastoral Care Code. The remaining question is whether it is consumer protection, consistent with the usage of the term in relation to Australia (Chapter Five). In his analysis of the Code, following Cerny (1997),

Lewis (2005) argues that New Zealand regulatory authorities have used the Pastoral Care Code as an ingredient in the broader strategy underpinning 'the competition state'. This represents:

> [T]he shift in national economic policy from managing the economy as an integrated fully constituted whole to a project of securing access to foreign markets, promoting international competitiveness and encouraging inward foreign investment. In enforcing outcomes that emerge from world markets and displacing the national cultural project with macroeconomic abstractions such as national competitiveness or more targeted interventions, it is one overt expression of the intersection of globalisation discourses and neo-liberal statecraft. (Lewis, 2005, p 19)

The link between international education as an export, the trade dimension, is clear in policy. The translation of the relationship between the government, and the 'industry' which the government seeks to foster, is not problem-free. One of the staff interviewees was well placed to comment on the tensions inherent to the competition state:

> 'There is quite a tension at the moment between the industry and the government. I think it's quite a fundamental issue, and the Code of Practice is part of that.... Thanks, government! You can help with the policy environment and on labelling [the regulatory] framework and trade settings and stuff like that. But beyond that, quite frankly, we're okay!' (NZ 9)

Yet another drew a link between market share and the avoidance of poor welfare outcomes, such as well-known incidents that resulted from crime and violence against international students in Australia. Drawing on the Canberra example of a Chinese student who was murdered and whose body was left for months before she was recognised, one New Zealand staff interviewee noted:

> '[T]hey [New Zealand authorities] started to realise that maybe they needed to do something so that they didn't get the same sort of incidents [as occurred in Australia]. And so that helped them start using the Code a little more.' (NZ 1)

Regardless of the nature of the relationship between the state and the industry, however – whether sometimes conflictual or always supportive – international education regulation through the New Zealand Code is designed first and foremost to help the nation-state to compete internationally.

Conclusion

Students, and parents in some cases, who take the time to do even a small amount of background research on education destination countries may credibly view New Zealand as an attractive study destination. It houses a generally safe, liberal, accepting culture that welcomes international students. Educational institutions and the national government, as with most institutions and governments in exporter countries, are always keen to promote this image of international education to outsiders. In this sense Australia is not at all different to New Zealand. Those who are particularly diligent and perhaps more risk-averse might read the Pastoral Care Code, or parts of it, as part of their 'try before you buy' research, or maybe as part of post-purchase information-seeking. It is in this dimension that New Zealand seems different to Australia. On the basis of the non-empirical parts of this chapter, the discussion of the formal regulations may substantiate the construction of New Zealand as a favourable overseas sojourn. All in all, if the student experience is favourable this may be an appropriate summation and there is little more to the research problem.

However, international education regulation is a process not only of protecting students. As much as any other function it may have, it is a process in global image management. The discussion of New Zealand in this chapter suggests that the Pastoral Care Code, in using the language of pastoral care, appears to be attractive in the sense of student-protective. It may be that New Zealand regulators and policy makers are better than their Australian counterparts in overseas marketing and/ or in the drafting of the Code. That has not been tested as a research problem. It cannot be ascertained from the current research, and it is not a conclusion we can draw. We can, however, argue on the basis of the interview data analysed in this chapter, that New Zealand appears quite similar to Australia in terms of student and staff perceptions of the regime. Rather than a superior programme, we find that on the ground, 'where the rubber hits the road', it is more a case of a great deal of regulation of favourable appearance but with little extra protection than Australia.

As argued, one source of our disquiet is the lack of accurate information flow from regulator, to institution, to student. However, there are other sources, to be more fully revealed in comparative analysis. It is the next chapter that interrogates more directly the primary comparison points between the two national programmes.

Note

[1] New Zealand interviewees are prefaced with 'NZ' for a service provider/ policy informant, and with 'S' for students'.

SEVEN

Different frameworks, similar outcomes: comparing Australia and New Zealand

Introduction

The broader regulatory environment of international education in New Zealand seems more settled than that in Australia. Racism, at least in relation to discrimination against incoming students, is a different and currently less pressing problem there. Government is more sturdy in its regulatory role and the export challenge posed by significant currency appreciation on world financial markets is less problematic in New Zealand, although the ongoing global financial crisis has had a far lower impact in Australia. Educationally and administratively substandard vocational colleges have been a greater problem for Australia. As discussed in this chapter, this is partly due to the existence of the IEAA in New Zealand. The international education–migration nexus is also a more pressing issue for Australian authorities. New Zealand did not undergo the same sharp drop in prospective student applications as occurred in Australia in 2009 and 2010. Over the last decade the overall growth of the international education market has been greater in New Zealand, since recovering from the market downturn from China (see Chapter Four, this volume), although New Zealand started from a lower base than Australia.

What of the central instruments that directly regulate international education? Australia's ESOS Framework and New Zealand's Pastoral Care Code outwardly display divergent features, with the Australian programme being based on consumer protection and the New Zealand legislation using the language of pastoral care. Staff and policy interviewees largely agreed with this distinction in the letter of the law, although few spoke in detail of the substance and significance of the difference. Students had little basic knowledge in this domain. However, more importantly and on deeper comparative interrogation, in both regimes the higher up and more influential the staff informant, the less in touch they were with the realities of regulation and student welfare deficits in practice. As argued in this chapter, the gulf between legislative language on the one hand, and the realities of student lived experience of that language on the other, becomes key to understanding the need for a cross-jurisdictional comparative approach.

On the ground and in practice we find that the Australian and New Zealand programmes are characterised more by similarity than by difference. The central basis of the similarity lies in the simultaneous pursuit by the two governments of international education strategies consistent with the overriding agenda of the 'competition state' (Cerny, 1997; Lewis, 2005). With international competitiveness as the main inspiration, student welfare takes a back seat, becoming derivative of the perceived need of the national economy to be a competitive entity rather than the nation-state being an agent of wellbeing. Accordingly it is suggested that there is a need for more comparative analysis in international education literature if scholars and policy makers are to better understand the welfare impact of regulation.

The first section of this chapter sets the context for comparison by reviewing relevant aspects of the comparative history of social policy and regulation in Australia and New Zealand. The second section examines the similarities and differences between the two formal frameworks, ESOS in Australia and the Pastoral Care Code in New Zealand. The third section continues the comparative analysis, but with reference to the student and staff interview data. Finally the chapter discusses the key themes that emerge from the totality of the comparison.

Comparative evolution of welfare

In the broad comparative sweep Australia and New Zealand are similar societies, both being former British colonies with English as their official language, and both originally being populated by non-European and non-Western Indigenous peoples. Today, although Australia is more economically successful due mainly to an ongoing boom in mineral exports, both are advanced economies with similar economic institutions. They also have exceptional, and similar, public and social policy histories (Castles, 1985; Ramia, 1998). As well as being allies politically and socially they have also been economic competitors in the international market, as discussed earlier in Chapter Four.

In terms of a national regime of 'social protection' as first conceived by Polanyi (1944), and as discussed in Chapter Two, historically both Australia and New Zealand approached the question of domestic or local student welfare through the regulatory prism of a distinctive welfare state, referred to by some social policy scholars as a 'wage-earners' welfare state' (see especially Castles, 1985; also 1988, 1989, 1992, 1994, 1996, 1997; Castles and Pierson, 1996; Castles et al, 1996). According to this model, social protection was pursued using four interlocking regulatory planks: arbitrated minimum employment conditions to protect workers; selective inward migration, perceived as a means to avoid migrants who would accept lower than Australasian-standard wages and working conditions; industry protection as the main economic incentive for employers to maintain labour conditions; and a market-oriented, 'residual' state welfare system designed as a last-resort safety net for those (mainly males) whose living standards were not otherwise protected.

In *Working class and welfare*, the originator of the wage-earners welfare model, Francis Castles (1985), argued that the policy pattern that characterised the two countries' social protection regimes for much of the 20th century was built on four interdependent policy planks. First, both established the world's only nationally applicable compulsory arbitration systems. These were the institutional mechanisms for providing worker protection through minimum wages and working conditions. Second, industry protection gave employers strong economic incentives to adhere to the minimum labour standards. Third, selective immigration policies were used as a means to exclude migrant workers entering from countries that had lower than Australasian-standard wages and conditions. By design, as well as being motivated by racial discrimination typical of the time, selectivity in immigration was a tool to avoid downward pressure on labour remuneration. Fourth, a comparatively early but minimalist and residual state welfare system was developed in both countries, relying first on a combination of the market and the family and second on a last-resort safety net in the form of state-provided welfare benefits and services.

The significant point about this history is that given the marketing of international education opened up in the 1980s in Australia, and the 1990s in New Zealand, international students in both countries were not subject to this social policy history. But what about the restructured welfare state during the period of international education expansion? Given the increasing intensity of competition that comes with globalisation, since the 1980s traditional European approaches to social protection have been rethought and in many cases restructured (Pierson, 2001; Katzenstein, 2003; cf Gilbert, 2002). Change in Australia and New Zealand, however, has been more transformational. Whereas most European states took until the 1990s to begin their restructuring in earnest, Australasia's social protection pattern did not last long into the 1980s. Over the 1970s and 1980s debate in the two countries centred on how to curb, if not reverse, welfare state expenditures. In addition, many governments began to pay greater attention to the OECD's quest to make welfare 'receipt' more 'active' and less 'passive', pressuring or compelling unemployed people to undertake labour market and training programmes (OECD, 1988, 1989, 1990).

Until the mid-1990s, however, Australian policy makers pursued activisation much more vigorously than their New Zealand counterparts. The activisation agenda would involve restructuring traditional methods of service and benefit delivery. From the labour market side, workplaces have been restructured so as to be more 'flexible' – again an OECD agenda (OECD, 1986a, 1986b) – designed to aid labour markets to adapt to continuing shifts in international demand. In sum, the postwar social protection tradition in Australia and New Zealand has been undone. The four-pronged approach of the wage-earners welfare model has been disintegrated and replaced by arrangements broadly consistent with individuals gaining protection from the vicissitudes of the market, ironically, through greater participation in the market. Many comparative and local policy analysts of Australia and New Zealand have captured this transition, albeit using varying language (see especially Bray and Haworth, 1993; Kelsey, 1993, 1995; Castles, 1996; Castles et al, 1996; Wailes, 2003; Ramia and Wailes, 2006).

The opening up of international education to the global market places international students squarely within the arena of market participation, rather than being welfare subjects. As discussed, over the period since the 1980s both Australia and New Zealand have been taking increasing numbers of international students, to the point of both becoming world players in the education market, in the absolute and relative senses. Coincident with the expansion of international education in Australia and New Zealand was the broader policy remodelling in response to global economic change (Wailes, 2003). Once the colonies were left to fend for themselves on international trade markets, and once the pressures of globalisation began to affect their economies in increasingly unpredictable ways, the overriding policy response of marketisation was deemed by national policy authorities to be inevitable. Although marketisation had different institutional characteristics in each country, from the early-to-mid 1980s the overarching shift toward 'economic liberalism' (Polanyi, 1944, p 132) formed the common backdrop to broader changes in the basis of social protection.

The expansion of international education began in this era, and continues in the current era of global economic change. Accordingly, to use a common Anglo analogy, student welfare as a policy concern began from behind the eight ball, and it is not moving forward. And as welfare subjects, international students are constructed using much the same foundations in the two countries.

From the 1980s to the early 1990s the regimes were different in that their programmes were conducted within different time frames and with different levels of severity in the shift towards marketisation. New Zealand was the more radical model, with a change process that was at once speedier and more extensive (see especially Bray and Haworth, 1993; Castles et al, 1996). Despite the major divergence during that period, however, there has been a re-convergence since the mid-1990s. Australia has moved closer to New Zealand in some key respects, and did so particularly emphatically under the John Howard-led Coalition government; and New Zealand's Labour government, first elected in 1999 but replaced with the conservative National Party in 2008, arguably moved back from the forefront of economic liberalism to meet Australia half-way (Ramia and Wailes, 2006).

Where did the international education programmes of the two countries fit within this broader policy context?

ESOS Framework versus the Pastoral Care Code

The previous two chapters have suggested that the broader regulatory environment of international education in New Zealand is more stable than that in Australia. The Pastoral Care Code has not undergone the same scale of change as its ESOS counterpart, and there are several reasons for this. First, formal regulation has a partly reputational function that is useful in the international market, but this function has less work to do in New Zealand. In Australia issues of personal safety of onshore students have been destabilising and have triggered the need for official diplomatic action. In recent years the associated problem of racism affecting some groups of international students – both perceived and manifestly real – has either been of a lower magnitude in New Zealand, or less well reported, and has not triggered public questions of racial discrimination to the same extent as in Australia.

New Zealand's government has seen less need for major change in international education policies, and nor has it experienced an appreciation of its currency, affecting the competiveness of exports, on the same scale as Australia (Watt, 2011). Australia's continuing economic strength, mainly resulting from its natural mineral resources, its capability in extracting those resources and their central role in supplying energy to China, Japan and Korea, is a double-edged sword. It has overriding economic benefits but it simultaneously places greater financial pressures on international students with effectively higher prices. Both regimes have been affected by the export downturn associated with the financial crisis, current to the time of writing, but as noted, international student enrolments appear more robust in New Zealand.

Another challenge which is somewhat greater for Australia than New Zealand is that posed by poor-standard vocational colleges. This is due in part to the existence and operation of the IEAA. In an interview, a pivotal senior figure in New Zealand cited personal experience of the IEAA as having the classic regulatory effect of amending the behaviour of educational institutions on student welfare matters (NZ 1). There is little evidence of an equivalent effect stemming from the operation of the ombudsmen at Commonwealth and state levels in existence in Australia. Associated with the issue of educational standards in vocational colleges, the Australian government has been more at pains than its New Zealand counterpart to tighten its regulation of the international education–migration nexus, as the vocational sector provides the clearest instance of students seeing opportunities for migration through education, over and above the professional value of the education services themselves.

The difference between the ESOS Framework and the Pastoral Care Code that is of greatest salience, however, lies in the language used and the ethos created, whether purely literal or substantive. Aside from the obvious usage of pastoral care in the New Zealand case and its absence in the Australian programme, the wording adopted by the relevant government agency of each country is different. The New Zealand Ministry of Education (2011a) states in its online introduction to the Code, which it administers:

> The Code of Practice advises education providers on the standards of care that they must provide to international students living and studying in New Zealand. The Code of Practice for the Pastoral Care of International Students (the Code) provides a framework for education providers to ensure a high standard of care and wellbeing is maintained for international students while they live and study in New Zealand.

Australian Education International (AEI, 2011), states in its counterpart description:

Australia has a reputation as a safe, progressive and dynamic place to study, and we maintain this reputation by providing quality education and consumer protection specifically developed for overseas students. The Education Services for Overseas Students (ESOS) Act 2000 and associated legislation are the legal framework governing the responsibility of education institutions towards overseas students.

Whereas the emphasis of the former is on words such as 'care' and 'wellbeing', Australian ESOS documentation mentions 'safety' but is replete with references to student recourse to refunds in the case of non-delivery or proven sub-standard delivery of a course. For example, it makes more of the imperative to protect student funds, and 'ensuring students get what they paid for'. Further:

The ESOS legislation requires all education institutions to enter into a written agreement with overseas students when they enrol. The agreement must specify a student's entitlement to a refund in cases of both provider and student default. For further information about consumer protection please refer to the consumer protection pages of AEI Online. (AEI, 2011)

An online link is provided to the consumer protection pages. An important and additional point lies in the reference there, within the pages of information on consumer protection regulations in relation to international education and quality assurance, to independent grievance mechanisms introduced within the last year to the time of writing, including the overseas students ombudsman as discussed earlier in Chapter Five. On the other hand, in New Zealand reference to the IEAA as an independent grievance avenue is significantly more prominent.

Despite this distinction and associated linguistic differences, what do the student and staff interview data suggest? Investigation of this is consistent with the emphasis of the book on the need for verification or otherwise of formal regulation. This is not merely to assess the impact of informal regulation as discussed in the previous two chapters, but in addition to probe broader experiences of the formal provisions and clauses.

Comparative data analysis

Taking Australia's ESOS Framework and New Zealand's Pastoral Care Code as the central formal regulation instruments, the two regimes outwardly display divergent paths. Pastoral care reflects the New Zealand approach and consumer protection the central motivation of the Australian approach. The fieldwork backs up this linguistic distinction, with almost all New Zealand staff interviewees speaking of pastoral care of international students as reflecting the ethos of the Code, while almost all their Australian counterparts spoke of the ESOS Framework in terms of providing protection to students consistent with the construction of that group as purchasers of a commercial service. Yet more importantly, a commonality between the regimes lies in the principle, also borne out by staff data, that the higher up and more influential the staff informant, the less in touch they are with the realities of regulation and the experience of it. The previous two chapters reflected on this question. On interrogating formal regulation alongside interview data, it becomes manifest that the difference in legislative language is not reflected in the lived experiences of international students.

This is mainly because students do not have sufficient information to render the difference substantive by accessing greater rights. The onus is on policy makers and educational institutions to ensure effective communication from government, to institution, to student; and students have a responsibility to be more proactive in acting on the protections afforded them. The problem of information inadequacies is fundamental, with its importance nowhere more clearly manifested than in the capacity of the IEAA to be effective in altering the behaviours of institutions for the betterment of welfare. The key, however, is that like any progressive agent, the IEAA is only effective in its role if the regulated agents are aware of it and take available opportunities to access it as and when needed. The key is to ask, as the next section of the chapter does, the deeper cross-national comparative question of why the information inadequacies may exist, and in whose interests it may be to uphold their continuation, even or especially if this results in student welfare deficits.

On the question of the general emphasis of rights provided by the national regulatory regime, the perceptions of Australian and New Zealand interviewees differed markedly. The most appropriate group to compare is the service provider employees at universities, who deal on an everyday and frontline basis with the experiences of students. University staff were also more able than students to provide such a perspective. The ESOS Act and the National Code in Australia were seen by staff almost entirely in terms of consumer protection and quality assurance, with academic and 'classroom' issues being central (for example, Oz 1).[1] Pastoral care was not a strong theme and issues in the broad terrain of social citizenship were all but absent. When asked for a general impression of the purpose of the Act and the National Code, one university interviewee replied:

'It [sic] is in essence a piece of, has two fundamental purposes: consumer protection for prospective students who have to buy before they try, and part of what I call ... the pillars of the Australian quality framework.... So consumer protection and quality assurance in that big picture realm for me.' (Oz 7)

On the other hand, consistent with the greater formal specificity and range of rights issues in New Zealand's Pastoral Care Code, provider staff in that country had more detailed responses and found it difficult to typify the approach in one or two concepts, as did their Australian counterparts. As one New Zealand service provider interviewee noted:

'[With the Pastoral Care Code] there is some kind of framework, some standard that the university is expected to adhere to; that is not a hodge-podge of different levels of service and things like that. And it's kind of like, the spin-off from it has been that the support services in different universities have managed to get together and talk about these issues.... [T]he code has given us a centre to some degree for the support network [for students].' (NZ 11)

Staff employed in the education ministries of the two countries replicated this basic difference between frameworks. Like the university employees, one ministry interviewee engaged in the administration of the ESOS Act and the National Code specified clearly that the Australian framework was one combining consumer protection and quality assurance (Oz 1); a counterpart employee in New Zealand spoke of the Pastoral Care Code in terms of general student welfare:

'[The Code gives us] a set of standards which are mandatory, [which] I think has given institutions [providers] the power to help the students and look after their welfare to a much

better extent than before [the introduction of the Code].'
(NZ 7)

Consistent with the perception of greater range and specificity in student protections in New Zealand, the existence of the IEAA, which has no Australian equivalent, was generally viewed favourably by New Zealand staff interviewees of all categories, incorporating those employed by the ministry (NZ 2, 3, 7, 8), the universities (NZ 4, 5, 6, 10, 11), the main cross-border education organisation (NZ 9) and the IEAA itself (NZ 1). The IEAA employee (NZ 1) emphasised that, with exceptions, the organisation was independent and – significantly from the regulatory point of view – was effective in altering behaviour among providers. This implies that universities would act less diligently in relation to student rights at various stages of the education service provision process in the absence of such an authority. For example, in referring to the case of a dispute over university fees, the employee reflected:

> '[W]hen I got the complaint I referred it back to the university and said, "Has this been through your internal grievance procedure? If it hasn't, could you please start that process?" Because no one quite knew what the internal grievance procedure of the university was, when the decision had been made by the university council what it might be. So at that point the university decided to set up an internal grievance procedure ... and the university pulled in its head. Now I'm sure that the existence of the Code must have been a significant feature of the university pulling in its head.' (NZ 1)

Here, as with levels of awareness of and about regulations, student data provides the most illuminating evidence. Students clearly rely on self-regulation of life opportunities, principally through their own support networks. Using 'loneliness' as an indicator of welfare deficit, of the 200 student interviewees in Australia, 65 per cent reported being lonely. Similarly, of 70 students in New Zealand, 65.7 per cent reported being lonely. Of the various sources of replacement security – including family, close friends and partners, casual friends and student representative NGOs and less formal or social organisations – students in both countries received greatest support via casual friends from among their fellow international students, totalling 90 per cent in New Zealand and 100 per cent in Australia from those who reported loneliness. A mixed picture emerges when close friends and partners and other groups are compared, and hence no further firm conclusions may be drawn. A more detailed picture of these is provided in Table 7.1.

Table 7.1: Comparison of students' networks in Australia and New Zealand

	Australia		New Zealand	
	Students Lonely *n* = 130	Students Not lonely *n* = 70	Students Lonely *n* = 46	Students Not lonely *n* = 24
Networks and associations include:	%	%	%	%
Immediate family.relatives	28	35	22	8
Close friends including boy/girl friends	60	51	87	83
Casual friends: other international students	100	76	90	100
Casual friends: local students	60	51	61	71
Social organisations	56	34	35	42

Informal networks of these kinds clearly play a role in filling some of the welfare gaps. In analysing cross-border education regulation in general and the New Zealand regime in particular, there is a need to examine whether less centralised regulations as exist in Australia may be as effective in providing for rights. Australian policy staff charged with administration of the ESOS Act and the National Code were in little doubt that their arrangements were both adequate and superior to their New Zealand counterparts in their contribution to student rights and security (Oz 1, 5, 6). For Australian interviewees the New Zealand model was largely inappropriate in the context of the former country's federal governmental system, given that responsibilities in many spheres are shared and negotiated between the state and Commonwealth levels (Oz 1).

However, in general neither New Zealand nor Australian staff interviewees had high levels of strategic or operational knowledge of the regime across the Tasman Sea from them. The exception was one New Zealand interviewee (NZ 9), who had previously worked within the (then) Australian Department of Education Science and Training (DEST) directly on the ESOS Framework and so had experience in both national systems. Being well qualified to provide comparative reflection, this interviewee's perspective was that ESOS was, as a formal regulatory instrument, more 'heavy-handed' in regulating education institutions than the New Zealand Code. More fully:

'We've [New Zealand regulators] looked quite closely at the ESOS Act and all of the other documentation around that. I think if it works well for Australia, good stuff. I was actually involved in drafting the original [New Zealand] Code of Practice and setting it up, and the Appeal Authority back in 1995 when I was working for the [New Zealand] Ministry of Education. At the time we deliberately went for a light-handed, also cost-effective way of implementing pastoral care. And that's where we came up with the Appeal Authority; it's like an ombudsman type of thing, that also protected the ... [interviewee pauses] It wasn't used to take a sledge hammer to the industry, which I think a lot of Kiwis perceive the ESOS Act to be. When we show people the ESOS Act and some of your [that is, Australian] discussion papers, it seems for a New Zealand context to be a bit over the top. And it might be [over the top] for a very small system like New Zealand. I mean, we are only the size of Melbourne, population-wise.

'But it [New Zealand Code] is significantly cheaper and that's where I think [interviewee pauses] ... I was working in DEST and we were cranking up ESOS and CRICOS [Commonwealth Register of Institutions and Courses for Overseas Students] charges and stuff like that, and some of the larger [educational] institutions seem to be paying a hell of a lot of money.' (NZ 9)

Although this may seem to contradict the Australian analysis in Chapter Five, it does not, in the sense that its finding was that the welfare content of ESOS was weak despite a comparatively prescriptive and wordy code. What the interviewee was picking up on was the codification and the relative expense of institutions' compliance in Australia. This is consistent with earlier findings.

It also connects with a methodological theme in comparative analysis that runs through this chapter; namely, that international education regulation does and must take into account the broader nation-specific institutional and political contexts. Even if the analyst or the casual observer were to prefer the more comprehensive pastoral care model of New Zealand over that of Australia, the shocks to the national system from within or outside the country cannot be ignored. Australia has had its own problems – financial ones that led to the establishment of the ESOS Act in 2000 and personal security-related problems – and New Zealand has had similar developments in relation to racist sentiment targeting students from China (McKenzie-McLean, 2007). An Australian policy maker interviewee referred to this when offering his explanation for the formation of the Pastoral Care Code (Oz 6). For him the response was prudent in terms of provider and national risk management. A New Zealand interviewee occupying an analogous position made a similar observation, although relating to New Zealand's episodes of racial targeting of Chinese students by the media and some members of the public (NZ 8).

Divergent formal regimes and similar data: comparative analysis

With formal regulatory frameworks indicating substantively different regimes and data analysis revealing that the divergence is exaggerated if not misleading in terms of student experience, how might reconciliation be sought? In other words, how might the analyst reliably compare Australia and New Zealand in light of both formal regulation and interview data, and what role is played by the informal realm? In finding the answers the first step is to identify the similarities and differences between the two regimes in the largely descriptive sense. Lest the importance of that be under-estimated, it is established that descriptive discussion is a vital pre-requisite to comparativism in scholarly analysis as comparativism is commonly conceived (Caramani, 2010). The historical comparison of the first section was an additional first step in contextualising contemporary regulation in the two countries. The value of historicism in internationalism and comparison has also been recognised (Mahoney et al, 2009). The second step, and the one which is at issue in this section, is the more conventional. It is that which defines the distinctive approach of the comparativist. It sits in addition to descriptive similarity and difference, and is the *explanation* of their *sources and causes*.

   The comparative policy and politics literature provides guidance on the conundrum posed by the coexistence of divergent formal regulation and similar data. As Geddes (2003) argues in her analysis of research design in comparativism, comparative analysis attracts different 'answers', depending on the question or questions being addressed, the cases chosen, the evidence contained in the cases and the research approach adopted. Research design is thus of central importance to any notion of accuracy and fairness of comparison. In the discussion of welfare evolution in the two countries, Australia and New Zealand have been compared across several public policy spheres in literature used and cited above. One clue to the matter is the two different approaches taken by scholars of comparative politics.

One approach, which can be called 'institutionalist', emphasises the role of national institutions in identifying and explaining similarities and differences, although this naturally tends towards an emphasis on difference given that the institutions of any nation follow an historical 'path dependence' and institutions rarely have identical features in more than one country, even if they have 'functional equivalence' or they serve the same or similar policy and regulatory objectives (Castles, 1989, 1992). Viewed in this light, for regulators as for scholars, the ESOS Framework and the Pastoral Care Code make simultaneously interesting and important comparators, although to repeat, using this approach leads the comparativist inexorably toward a bias in assessing formal frameworks. The bias comes to the neglect of underlying structural political-economic similarities between the two national cases. The second approach is that of theorists who emphasise such similarities, countering those 'new institutionalists' who emphasise difference. In relation to Australia and New Zealand, Wailes, Ramia and Lansbury (2003) review the main variant of this alternative in the so-called 'material interests' framework, which prioritises the international economic and political forces which push nations under conditions of ever-greater global integration toward increasing convergence (Rogowski, 1989; Swenson, 1991; Iversen, 1996). Central factors behind this convergence are cross-class alliances, and coalitions of business and state interests, whose agenda is to shape the policy, regulation and economic outcomes of the nation-state in the global context.

Similar reasoning in application to the analysis of international education regulation is seen in the construct of the 'competition state', which characterises the nation-state as an entity which must compete to advance its own interests in ways similar to business firms and empires (Cerny, 1997). Universities in major education exporter nations act essentially according to the strategic logic of trans-national corporations (Ramia et al, 2011). They focus increasingly on revenues generated from the sale of their educational services. As Lewis (2005) suggests in his analysis of New Zealand's Pastoral Care Code, the state can and does seek to maximise its export and competitive interests partly by formulating regulation regimes which pit educational institutions against each other in the search for ever-greater revenues, and nation-states against each other on a similar basis in the quest to maximise export dollars. In his framework the New Zealand Code is an instrument, the primary purpose of which is not pastoral care of international students, but the competitive maximisation of the state's opportunities in the global marketplace. In this argument the Code is multifaceted and sophisticated in its integration of various educational regulation instruments, but it is essentially the neoliberal expression of a government with a:

> ... management interest in the making of this globalising industry [international education]. A new Code of Practice [for the Pastoral Care of International Students] enacts multiple technologies of control from quality control to standard setting, benchmarking, certification and audit. Legitimated by a discourse of concern for the pastoral care of school-aged students, it requires institutions to provide detailed information. The Code makes "the industry" visible, makes a market, controls brand NZ education, regulates through consumer assurance, and imposes direct disciplinary controls on institutions. The Code of Practice makes apparent the ambitions and governmental technologies of the "augmented" neo-liberal state, and is a pivotal structure in the constitution of the industry and of the globalising processes that define it. (Lewis, 2005, p 5)

The connection of international education to neoliberalism and a focus on the 'industry' aspect of the educational services of New Zealand are key considerations. Pastoral care in such a frame is secondary to what for the government is more important and politically beneficial in neoliberal times: the international competitiveness of the nation-state itself.

This is a compellingly relevant argument for comparison of the New Zealand Code with Australia's ESOS Framework, given that the latter's designers, stakeholders and central gate-keepers each and all have explicitly constructed the regulations first and foremost in terms of protection of international public and economic image, and Fund insurance through a consumer protection edifice, rather than any well conceived notion of student welfare for its own sake. When this is considered alongside the evidence gathered through student data as analysed above, the experience of international students in assessing their welfare is much the same in Australia and New Zealand.

But who stands to benefit from this 'sameness'? Whose 'material interests' are furthered by the maintenance of students' ignorance, equally in both countries, of the statutory and administrative protections available to them? What lies behind the similarity of feedback from students in relation to the formal and informal sources of the welfare that they do enjoy? And what effectively explains the resulting, identifiable student welfare deficit in both countries?

Comparative analysis, taking into account both institutional and material interest logics, suggests that the latter must be closer to the truth, as long as the empirical dimension of the analysis decides on the controversy. There is a major weakness in comparative-institutional scholarship if it is conducted to the neglect of empirical evidence on important issues such as international student welfare. Differential formal provisions are not deterministic as long as detailed feedback from students and staff indicates that the differences are essentially not material for determining welfare.

This should not come as a surprise when considered in the context of the long historical record, as discussed in the first section of the chapter. The evolution of the two nations' social protection institutions and welfare outcomes over the last 120 years reveals periods of strong convergence, although also other periods of major divergence in policy trajectory. The two regimes were quite similar in the 1890s up to the First World War. This was the period during which they were both seen internationally as social innovators. Leading up to the Second World War and into the long economic boom of the postwar period New Zealand emerged as the welfare leader, distinguishing itself by creating elements of the world's first universally applicable social security and health programmes in particular. For much of the post-Second World War period, however, the two regimes fell behind social policy innovations in Europe. The 1980s and part of the 1990s was a period of major industry restructuring and adaptation to the pressures of economic globalisation, although New Zealand then took the path of more radical privatisation and social security cutbacks as well as cuts in various service areas of the welfare state. Education was part of that rolling back. As noted, since the mid-1990s they have, with few exceptions, become quite similar again as Australia moved, albeit more steadily than New Zealand had done, towards marketisation.

It is within this latter period, which takes in the time of writing, that international education has undergone its major expansion. The mass model of international higher education is new and historically unprecedented. In the sense of newness, international education does not represent devolving of responsibilities from the state to the market, but more the creation of markets as the major regulatory form of education. Based on the evidence presented here, that form appears to be similarly strong in each country.

Conclusion

The comparison of Australia's ESOS Framework and New Zealand's Pastoral Care Code suggests that there are major differences which are legally, and thus in a formal regulatory sense, substantive. That comparison is essentially between a consumer protection framework and pastoral care package. The distinction is linguistically significant, and enough to send information signals to international students in their own self-regulation. Staff interviewees by and large believed they were operating under systems that were consistent with this difference of terminology. Upon tapping and assessing the experiences of both students and staff informants, however, we found that the significance of the differences in the Codes must be questioned. Indeed the interview data revealed much the same overall welfare experience for students in each case, with a relationship between the formal and informal sources of welfare that was close to identical. In empirical assessment of the Codes, the need to conduct fieldwork with international students, and not just staff, has been established. As a result of this assessment the potency of formal regulation has been held up for questioning.

The evidence of staff working under each regime differed, based partly on their level of connectedness to service provision for students. That is, the closer they were to the coalface of service provision, the more they identified problems. Yet the student data did not reveal differences between their experiences that could be deemed of comparative significance. This was partly because students in both countries had poor levels of knowledge about the protections that were available to them, and partly because of lack of effective communication of information by government and universities. The IEAA as independent umpire in New Zealand matters in important ways for those who use it, but the poor information provision and institutional communication with students limits its regulatory potency in practice. Too many students do not know of its existence, let alone its major legal powers and significant mandate.

The central point of this chapter, however, is that similarity in the comparison prevails over difference. The comparative analysis accordingly raises fundamental questions for regulation theorists. Given that, as discussed earlier (in Chapter Two), regulation is designed or deemed by its adherents to be deterministic of important social and economic outcomes, the inability of the ESOS Framework and the Pastoral Care Code to differentiate themselves in ways consistent with their differential language is something of a mystery. The perceived need by each state to pursue the strategies of the competition state come at the expense of student welfare. The market comes in more than one regulatory guise, but it is its character as a market that prevails, and we find that comparativism prevails over regulation theory when it comes to understanding international student welfare.

Note

[1] Australian interviewees are prefaced with 'Oz' for service provider/policy informants

EIGHT

Doing it differently: national and global re-regulation and trans-national student citizens

What are the prospects for regulation in Australia and New Zealand from this point? What needs to be done at the national level and what are the possibilities in the trans-national arena? With student and staff interview data in respect of each regime effectively working against the idea that the two are substantively different to each other in terms of the welfare impact of formal regulation, whether national regulation 'matters' is an important question. On the other hand, similarity of comparative outcomes increases the likely utility of similar re-regulation. The comparative reform project is, in practice, made easier if the outcomes, actual and desired, are similar in the two countries. As argued here, however, in principle a fundamental additional consideration is that the national context cannot be fruitfully reformed without simultaneous attention to levels above and beyond the ambit of the nation-state. The trans-national and the global arenas are called into play.

Formal regulation in the trans-national sphere shows the potential to have an impact on the national, but it is yet to be comprehensively tested because the conduct of so few nations has been substantively affected by it when it comes to education. The central global instrument designed to free up trade and create global convergence in international education regulation, the WTO's GATS, is almost (although not quite) significant if assessed by the number of signatories. Yet the number of countries whose activities are meaningfully affected or amended by it is small. The scope for *informal* regulation is a more interesting and fruitful question because it has greater potential to teach researchers and regulators lessons geared towards enhanced student welfare.

Given the need for reform at the national level, and the inability of Australian and New Zealand regulators to meaningfully provide welfare through existing means – at least not without the revamped political will of all regulatory agents including students themselves – this chapter argues that re-regulation should encompass a combination of revised national arrangements leading towards a national student citizenship. Due to the absence of a citizenship agenda, this involves a major re-conception of the status of international students. Importantly, however, in addition the analysis calls for a fresh vision of the trans-national aspects of that citizenship. This is similarly revolutionary, but it is necessary, with the available literature suggesting that in the context of globalisation, the global and national levels are indivisible in questions of reform. In addition, conceptually regulation must be married with citizenship, although the dearth of direct scholarly explorations of the nexus between the two constitutes a hurdle. Finally, given the highly commercialised nature of Australian and New Zealand higher education, a challenge is presented by the need to reconcile international market competition with the kinds of trans-national cooperation required for effective global regulation.

The first section of this chapter discusses reform-focused activities at the national level, incorporating the formal and informal regulatory spheres. The second section does the same for the global level. In the third section the chapter discusses the student rights dimension of the global–national nexus through the concept of trans-national citizenship. Part of this task is to conceive regulation and citizenship in their national and trans-national forms, exploring the problems with and the prospects for a marriage between them for the sake of enhanced student welfare. Finally, in light of the discussion of citizenship, the fourth section puts forward reform options for both the national and global levels.

Reform-focused activity at the national level

As revealed in Chapter Five, the most significant regulatory problem in Australia is that the consumer protection framework underpinning the ESOS Framework, although extensive, is largely non-specific and non-effectual as an instrument for the provision of student welfare. Although the chapter revealed a seemingly vibrant debate incorporating several government fora at the federal and state levels, and despite a debate surrounding the possibility of establishing an independent education umpire or similar body, little has eventuated to substantively change the lived experiences of students in higher education. Having said that, it should be acknowledged that an international student ombudsman has been created within the office of the Commonwealth ombudsman. This specifically covers vocational college students by providing an avenue for complaint outside and above the educational institution level. The fact that this body is not transparently domiciled as having its own, independent existence outside of the Commonwealth ombudsman – and the fact that it is as yet not clear how sharp are its regulatory teeth

– suggests that the situation is at best a case of 'wait and see' before assessing effectiveness.

It is important to note that even if an effective ombudsman that covered all international students were to be established in Australia, it would only take that regime to the point where New Zealand is already. It is also worth recalling that the IEAA in that country serves the purpose of an ombudsman, and has done so to significant effect on the conduct of educational and other institutions for those students who have accessed it. As found in Chapter Six, however, those students accessing the IEAA are limited in number when it is considered that relatively few of them showed knowledge of the IEAA's very existence, let alone its protective role. Hence it can be recalled that New Zealand's major regulatory problem is that, despite having a long-established pastoral care framework as the basis for its Code, many of the protections are mysterious to students, and information flow remains a significant barrier. International students in both Australia and New Zealand face major challenges in being recognised as welfare subjects, with neither the consumer protection of the former, nor the pastoral care of the latter, doing the job.

Yet there are developments in each country that give some cause for optimism. In Australia, for example, as well as the somewhat fertile policy debate in the area as discussed in Chapter Five, currently the Human Rights Commission, peak higher education body Universities, Australia, and the Academy of Social Sciences in Australia have combined with academics in efforts to address student wellbeing as a problem, and in particular human rights and racism, through workshops and research-based discussion papers (Graycar, 2010; Jakubowicz with Monani, 2010). The Human Rights Commission has also made efforts to provide important information and outreach to international students (AHRC, 2011). International students have set up their own public fora, some of which are on video and/or online (ustream, 2011), with projects canvassing issues specifically important to female international students (VIWRC, 2011), and other student groups aiming 'to sharpen safety skills' among their own ranks (Think Before, 2011). In addition, traditionally active student representative organisations remain on watch to make important contributions to public awareness of international education issues and to provide advice to international students. These include the Australian Federation of International Students (AFIS), the Council of International Students Australia (CISA), the National Union of Students (NUS) and the Council of Australian Postgraduate Associations (CAPA) (see, for example, NUS, 2010; AFIS, 2011; CAPA, 2011). Among the culturally specific student organisations, the Federation of Indian Students of Australia (FISA, 2011) stands out as being most active, particularly in the wake of racist attacks against Indian students in recent years.

In November 2009 the Australian and New Zealand Race Relations Roundtable met with relevant academics and international student representatives to explore issues of racism against international students, subsequently issuing a Roundtable Communiqué (AHRC, 2011). This recognised that student safety, while the most publicly prominent issue, is itself symptomatic of 'other issues' (AHRC, 2009), which include:

> [D]iscrimination, the lack of accessible and affordable accommodation, poor employment conditions, transport costs, lack of student support services, variable quality of education, and social isolation and exclusion. (AHRC, 2009)

Importantly, international student informants made Roundtable commissioners:

> [A]ware of the importance of seeing the students not as cash cows, but as global citizens and Australian residents. Up to 40% of students are engaged in the workforce and around 20% go on to become permanent residents with a wide range of skills and qualifications. (AHRC, 2009)

The Communiqué made clear its resolutions, all of which go to the heart of the regulatory issues addressed generally in this book and specifically in the remainder of this chapter. Verbatim quoting is thus not only justified but also necessary (see AHRC, 2009). The commissioners resolved to:

- Highlight the treatment of international students as a major current human rights and race relations issue and stress the importance in any response of addressing it from a human rights perspective;
- Note that the harassment and abuse of international students cannot be adequately addressed if the existence of racism as a significant factor is denied;
- Call for more research into the actual experience of discrimination and harassment of international students in specific communities and contexts, including regular surveys of students by education providers to provide a better evidence base for policy decisions;

- Call on the police to record complaints and incidences of racially motivated crime, and for education providers, local government and other stakeholders to provide accessible reporting systems for racial harassment and discrimination, including web-based systems;
- Encourage the provision of reliable and accessible web-based information to prospective international students, including about their human rights and support available;
- Monitor progress in addressing the human rights of international students and support students' organisations in their advocacy and support for an improved experience for international students in Australia and New Zealand;
- Increase public awareness of the rights of international students, their contribution to the Australian and New Zealand economies and societies, and the importance of speaking out when they witness instances of harassment, discrimination and abuse;
- Continue to engage with stakeholders on the rights of international students' networks and forums. (AHRC, 2009)

In New Zealand, despite the more settled nature of the international education debate as noted in Chapters Six and Seven, the safety of international students has featured in its Human Rights Commission fora and has gained significant attention from the race relations commissioner (NZHRC, 2011a, 2011b). This was arguably most directly prompted by the need to avoid the kinds of violent, racist attacks experienced by international students in Australia. The New Zealand Human Rights Commission's interest also stems partly from calls for the country to implement the UN International Covenant on Economic, Social and Cultural Rights, by the UN Committee bearing the same title (NZHRC, 2010).

It is clear from the Communiqué of the Race Relations Roundtable that, for the nation-state to be able to effect reform with respect to student welfare – in this case Australia and New Zealand, but in principle, any state – the nexus between the national and global regulatory arenas cannot be separated. The experiences of students who cross national borders for the purpose of study in a country that is not the one they call home are the product of both home and host country experiences. Particularly for those who study onshore in countries with vastly different cultures and language, the experience can be an isolating one, but nevertheless one which is affected by more than one country.

Global level

International education is a decidedly trans-national phenomenon. With this in mind it is necessary to ask questions of the global regulatory instruments and actors in the arena of international education. It has been noted in Chapter Two that the WTO's GATS has always had the potential to play a significant – and perhaps the primary – role in underpinning irreducible trans-national standards in relation to student welfare. Yet this potential is to date largely untried. The UN Education, Scientific and Cultural Organisation (UNESCO) plays a role which is similar in the sense of standard setting, although different in the sense that the standards are not in relation to trade but to education services themselves. Officially UNESCO (2011) 'works to create the conditions for dialogue among civilisations, cultures and peoples, based upon respect for commonly shared values.' Its central objective is access to as high a standard of education as possible, for all in the world. However, in practice much of UNESCO's work does not deal directly with international student welfare, other than to promote the UN's Millennium Development Goals (MDGs) and to play a role in the Universal Declaration of Human Rights. International students are human rights subjects, but enforcement is the same problem in education as it is in any area of the UN's work.

Beyond this UNESCO is a source of information to all potential and actual international students, mainly on questions of quality education and accreditation, with its Global Forum on International Quality Assurance, Accreditation and the Recognition of Qualifications. UNESCO also works, inter alia, on issues relating to trade in higher education, and open and distance learning, although much of its coverage of this dimension relates to the GATS agenda. The UN system more broadly, particularly through the International Labour Organization, has not played a significant part in advocating for the enforcement of international students' rights to fair treatment in part-time employment. The UN's 1990 International Convention on the Protection of the Rights of All Migrant Workers and Members of their Families excludes workers who are international students (see Cholewinski, 1997, Chapter 4). Little data exists on paid employment hours and remuneration levels for international students who work in the host country, although research suggests that working students form a significant category, with sizeable numbers working longer hours than is legally allowable under their visas. Exploitation appears to be relatively common (Nyland et al, 2009). Regional international governmental organisations (IGOs), such as the Asian Development

Bank, could equally play a larger role in protecting students, although it is yet to happen.

International education in general, and student welfare in particular, are noticeably absent from the agendas of other, prima facie, suitable organisational hosts for student matters at the global level. Like UNESCO, the International Organization for Migration (IOM) is an intergovernmental organisation, with a central commitment to 'the principle that humane and orderly migration benefits migrants and society' (IOM, 2011). The IOM has an interest in the main developments within the international education market (IOM, 2008, Chapter 4), but this is part of its broader interest in the phenomenon of migration rather than international education per se. It has little to say on the experiences or the wellbeing of students, other than as a group of trans-national migrants. Like UNESCO it interacts with GATS, although not so much in relation to international students, but rather, in relation to migrants who work in service provider roles (IOM, 2008, Chapter 1).

Outside of the intergovernmental sphere, and thus in the realm of the informal in global regulation, there is an entity called the International Student Movement (ISM). Despite the 'movement' in its title, this is not an organised social movement in the ordinary sense. Inaugurated in the University of Marburg in Germany as a collectivity of students it serves only as 'a communication platform used and shaped by groups of activists around the world struggling against the increasing privatisation of education and for free emancipatory education for all to share information, network and make coordinations' (ISM, 2013). ISM agitates against the commercialisation of global education and strives for universal access to education and against all forms of discrimination in, and in relation to, education, as well as for academic freedom and against some educational standards coordination instruments such as the Bologna process. This is largely because the Bologna process is geared towards labour market outcomes rather than access to education as such. ISM is highly conscious of the need to integrate the local–global nexus in its activist work:

> The impacts of the current global economic system create struggles worldwide. While applying local pressure to influence our individual local/regional politics and legislation, we must always be aware of the global and structural nature of our problems and learn from each other's tactics, experiences in organizing, and theoretical knowledge. Short-term changes may be achieved on the

local level, but great change will only happen if we unite globally. (ISM, 2013b)

Despite the potential to include questions of student welfare on the ground – which would not necessarily be against its stated mission – ISM does not incorporate such questions in its work. There remains the problem of the continuing absence of a united, global representative organisation of international students that works effectively towards student welfare.

National and global regulation: trans-national citizenship?

Given the regulatory impasse, how might the question of student welfare be more effectively catered for? This is first and foremost a practical question, of providing for rights typically through services. This aspect is discussed in the following section. However, before the practical aspects can be adequately addressed, there is an onus on reformers to address the theoretical question regarding the concept of student rights, based on the full recognition that international students traverse national borders and are thus in most ways different to their local counterparts, as discussed in Chapter Two.

Within traditional, state-centred notions of citizenship – the welfare dimension of which was first authoritatively explicated in T.H. Marshall's (1963) 'social rights of citizenship' – the primary relationship conferring rights within society is that between the state and the individual. This situates citizenship as a regulatory question. Yet regulatory perspectives – at least those that embrace non-traditional regulation concepts such as informal regulation – have rarely been used to analyse citizenship. The converse is also not common. Political sociologist Saskia Sassen (2002b, p 278) elevates the political dimension, arguing that at its base 'citizenship describes the legal relationship between the individual and the polity.' She embraces the global dimension of citizenship; indeed for her, that is indispensable. However, the state referred to by most scholars of citizenship is traditionally the *nation*-state. This is well established and need not be rehearsed here. In recent years Hansen (2009), among others, has reviewed and updated admirably the assumption that citizenship theory must have at its basis the nation-state for the establishment of rights, even if he questions the necessity of trans-national forms of citizenship, which we argue is indispensable in relation to welfare categories such as international students. From the other side of the debate and with a similar approach, Fox (2005) also comprehensively reviews the literature. He makes clear the case for understanding trans-national citizenship. His contention is that if the analyst seeks to define trans-national citizenship, they must first ask what 'counts' as trans-national citizenship.

Without seeking to settle the question, Fox draws on the crucial element of 'trans-national civil society' to put forward the case for a more rights-conducive 'globalisation from below'. Consistent with our analysis in general and the discussion of Chapter Two in particular, and translated for the interrogation of international students' rights, if the informal aspects of citizenship are included alongside the formal, in principle, trans-national citizenship is possible. For those who cross borders, at least for the term of their overseas education, there are more significant barriers to rights claims, let alone rights enforcement, than for those who claim within and in relation to the state to which they have formal, legal citizenship. We return to this argument below. With regard to the case for trans-national citizenship for international students one must continue with Fox (2005, p 175), who notes emphatically its limitations, yet argues with respect to the main approaches to understanding citizenship:

> If one extends the *vertical citizen-state relationship* transnationally, then the analogous reference point would be multilateral public authorities, such as the European Union, the United Nations, and the international financial and trade institutions, as well as new bodies such as the International Criminal Court. If one extends the more *society-based approach* to citizenship horizontally across borders, then the focus would be on membership in trans-national civic or political communities.... In an *actor-based approach*, membership in a political community is the key criterion. In a *rights-based approach*, the establishment of enforceable access to rights marks the threshold that determines citizenship. (Fox, 2005, p 175; emphasis added)

With globalisation in general – and manifestations of it such as the internationalisation of education in particular – the state must logically be partly replaced or pre-empted by trans-national public and civic actors. In other words, the role that it traditionally played is now increasingly taken on by other actors, many or most of which are trans-national. The most prominent of the actors are the kinds of IGOs identified in the previous section, although NGOs also have a role, while recognising that in relation to both kinds of organisations, the potential to play a progressive role is far from its realisation. Hence, in the struggle for student rights, with globalisation the state–individual relationship is usurped or at least supplemented by relations between IGOs, civil society and individuals.

To apply the various approaches put forward by Fox (2005), there must be a confluence of various developments. First, *actors* must work in more productive cooperation that is conducive to increasing student welfare. Second, further to the society-wide approach to citizenship, there needs to be active members of organisations and social and political movements that work towards better welfare. Third, consistent with enhanced *vertical relations between citizen and state* there should be more effective recognition and servicing of student rights by government and by non-state service-providing organisations, although the latter would constitute more horizontal forms of provision rather than vertical.

In principle this kind of cooperation stands to raise the standard of citizenship from trans-national, which implies the crossing or traversing of national borders, further towards a greater ideal, that of the cosmopolitan. Stemming from the Greek words for world, *kosmos*, and city, *polis* (Tomlinson, 1999, p 184), cosmopolitanism stems from the ideal of philosopher Immanuel Kant (for a secondary account of which see Kleingeld, 1998). It envisions the world as a federation of states rather than the extant disconnected and fractured collection of them. As a political project this involves concepts of equality, although it remains an ideal.

If it is believed that residents of a country are worthy of 'equality of status' – to invoke Marshall's (1963, p 107) original formulation, and/or in Polanyi's (1944, p 132) timeless words, 'social protection' from the 'deleterious action of the market' – the bases for excluding international students from citizenship remain an unanswered question for national policy makers. In the face of objections on the grounds that international students perhaps should not be eligible for citizenship, given that formal national citizens (here, local students) in developed Western countries have faced continual threats to the maintenance of their own rights, one must recall the differences in claimable rights between local and international students. As well as all of those discussed in Chapters One and Two, which need no repeating here, locals are at base still provided with a variety of administrative means of redress of injustice, which are not available to their international counterparts. Even where they are available there are well-documented barriers to access (Marginson et al, 2010). The social security arena provides a significant example (see, for example, CPAG 2008). Given the feedback of some policy staff interviewees in the analysis of this book, change to this situation appears neither politically likely nor persuasive as a reform option, let alone as a reform agenda.

The case is not lost, however, when the conceptual possibilities are considered. The society-based, actor-based and rights-based approaches, each and all, have the potential to form partial bases for a reform agenda. Despite continuing uncertainties in the general case, and despite the manifest failure of the Australian and New Zealand states in particular to offer a coherent student citizenship in practice, it is well established that the market share argument for student welfare is the most persuasive one in the context of competition states. The simple prescription is thus that, while it is unlikely that a comprehensive national citizenship-based reform agenda will be realised, recognition of the citizenship options can move the agenda forward. Consistent with the literature, however, the agenda is of necessity multipronged and multilevel, incorporating perspectives and actions that are global and local. It must be based on more coordinated national support structures. It should manage but eventually move beyond conceptual confusions in regulation and governance. The central and most difficult challenge to be faced, however, is how formal regulatory authorities move beyond the consumer protection and pastoral care mindsets and into welfare for its own sake.

National and global reform

Given the difficulties, what constitutes a realistic reform agenda that is consistent with the provision of post-national, trans-national citizenship? In a manner similar to other social arenas of global regulation, from aid and fair trade promotion to poverty alleviation and much in between (see especially Braithwaite and Drahos, 2000; Braithwaite, 2006), education has a fractured set of support structures.[1] The analysis of the Australian and New Zealand formal regulation regimes, combined with fieldwork with international students and staff and policy informants in the two countries, reveals several layers in the welfare programme. The layers are not organised in any particularly firm format, whether laterally or vertically, given that, as discussed above, trans-national regulation does not conform to either one in isolation from the other. Hierarchy features reinforcing 'globalisation from above', but so do more lateral formats and fora, 'globalisation from below' (Apple et al, 2005), or what could be seen as the positive harnessing the benefits of globalisation, principally through civil society advocacy and mobilisation (Fox 2005).

The first layer is the individual student her/himself. The second is the student's social and familial networks, including family and friends in the home and host countries. Then there is the university level including the services provided at that level, followed by the employer and the landlord or real estate agent, who has significant control over international student accommodation. There is also the host community, including formal cultural, faith- and interest-based non-profit organisations to which students may belong or associate. There are the agencies of the host government, and finally, there are global institutions, the IGOs and NGOs discussed previously, which typically have a higher level of formality but are to this point most detached from the student's everyday experience.

With the root of welfare residing in the individual student, students partly seek the benefits of international education in the host country through self-help. As this book's predecessor analysis, *International student security* (Marginson et al, 2010) reveals, however, loneliness and intercultural and language difficulties provide barriers to the realisation of individual capacities. Family and friendship networks help to fill voids, although, as well as receiving support, some students also have a strong onus to provide it back to family in the home country during the overseas candidature experience. This can take the form of money transfers but is often non-financial, connecting with the themes of the informal domain. Universities and other educational institutions provide services in many areas vital to welfare, including health and medical, employment, counselling and accommodation, although these services are most often difficult to coordinate with people and support structures outside the educational setting.

Indeed as we have found, coordination of services with community organisations both within and outside universities, and connection with employers and landlords, is one of the central difficulties in regulating student welfare. Formal, traditional command-and-control regulation by government is potentially effective in picking up some of the pieces, but the Australian government's ESOS Framework and New Zealand's pastoral care counterpart offer consumer protection and pastoral care at best, and thus neither meaningfully caters for students as social citizens. In this sense international students have simply not been furnished with comparable social and economic rights as formal citizens or permanent residents. The concurrently local and trans-national character of this citizenship context poses additional challenges.

Towards a more effective regime

In identifying the main features of an improved set of regulatory arrangements it must be acknowledged that the design of support structures has long been known to be limited in guaranteeing 'good governance' in national and trans-national settings (Held, 1995, 2004; Goodin, 1996). Yet key principles likely to furnish international students with better welfare can be put forward.

First, professional regulators – those whose official role it is to design formal regulation as discussed here – should combine the perspectives of regulation and governance in their practice, and should not be delayed or discouraged by the conceptual confusion between them in the social sciences literature. Second, there is a need to step up efforts to more effectively coordinate existing national support structures for better integration of the several layers or levels of student welfare discussed above. Third, although a complex principle and one that is difficult to implement, it is necessary to more effectively coordinate national with trans-national institutions. Fourth, regulators need to redesign programmes to construct international students as citizenship subjects rather than merely commercial education consumers or subjects of pastoral care. These four aspects are discussed in turn, the fourth being in the Chapter's Conclusion section, given its subsuming character

Combine regulation and governance

As argued in Chapter Two, the concepts of regulation and governance are easily and often conflated and their borders are intermalleable. Yet here there is an onus to put forward broad suggestions on how the two might be combined and/or have their borders clarified. The first and broadest principle to be applied is that professional regulators re-conceive existing regulation to incorporate governance into student welfare analysis. To reiterate from the discussion in Chapter Two, as argued by Braithwaite, Levi-Faur and Coglianese (2007, p 3) in their editorial for the journal *Regulation and Governance*, governance refers to provision, distribution and regulation. Being a subset of governance, regulation involves the 'steering [of] the flow of events', or put more simply, the affecting of behaviour among regulatory agents. Frederickson (2005, p 283) adds that governance includes the 'contextual influences that shape the practices of public administration.' This includes the harnessing and reinvention of relations with non-state, interjurisdictional and importantly non-jurisdictional actors such as IGOs and trans-national NGOs.

Agents in our analysis include each of those identified in the above discussion in relation to 'levels' of action: the individual student; the student's family and friends in home and host country; employers and landlords and real estate agents; the host community including organisations which students may associate with or belong to; the agencies and institutions of the host government; and finally, international institutions and organisations. If conceived as Braithwaite et al (2007) did, the governance perspective involves understanding the existing pattern of interaction between these, the interjurisdictional and interorganisational issues raised by security reform, the different and enhanced coordinated pattern needed for reform, and the need for more effective and student-centred service provision and distribution of life opportunities among international students and between students, local and international. The steering, distribution and provision aspects of regulation and governance need to be intermarried, with the command-and-control and less formal aspects incorporated.

Integrate national support structures

In the public administration literature in recent years a debate has been taking place, focusing primarily on the existence of a post-managerialist era in governance (see, for example, Alford, 2008; Rhodes and Wanna, 2009; Ramia and Carney, 2010). It is argued by some that governments in developed countries have moved beyond the excesses of commercial, 'new public management'-style programmes and towards the principles of 'public value' creation (Moore, 1995). Although the commercial criteria by which public service performance is assessed remain important, these are supplemented by more collectively defined, deliberative and more consultative and democratic means. Associated with this, and in addition, some argue that the old concept of the public official knowing best and thus defining in a top-down fashion the public 'good' or public interest, using the classic regulatory means of command and control, is gone. Although such traditional mechanisms remain, they are supplemented by more cross-agency and interministerial policy work through so-called 'whole-of-government' strategies (see, for example, MAC, 2004), and more consultation by government in the formulation of policy.

The argument that public value is prominent and real is interesting and important to contemporary regulation and governance, but it is not directly relevant here. The central point is that the establishment of public value concepts and agendas is consistent with the kinds of re-regulation called for in this book. Consultation with international students is potentially conducive to their improved welfare and rights recognition. The same can be said of the kinds of cross-agency work underpinning the 'whole of government' approach to policy and public services. Greater consultation and partnership with progressive student NGOs and social and political movements is also conducive to these ends.

There have been some developments consistent with such an agenda. For example, in Australia the creation of the collaboratively developed 'International Student Strategy' by the Council of Australian Governments (COAG, 2009) is a step in the right direction, COAG itself being an illustrative example of a whole-of-government forum. In the informal and formal spheres there is cooperation around schemes such as Think Before (2011), as discussed above. This increases awareness of student safety. The New Zealand government's work with UNESCO is also positive (NZHRC, 2010) in the process of integrating global with local regulation, and in Australia and New Zealand the work of the two Human Rights Commissions is to be applauded; in particular, recent partnerships with university academics, researchers and their representatives in the Academy of the Social Sciences in Australia, and Universities Australia (Graycar, 2010; Jakubowicz with Monan, 2010).

More can be done to use such fora to install more positive individual initiatives, which typically make governments more directly accountable for international student matters. Transport concession policies and public health coverage provide good examples. The relatively obvious and administratively easy regulatory steps towards reform include the establishment of transport concessions where they do not already apply, and making the public healthcare system free and in line with the coverage of local students. The UK already does this for its internationals. Building from these kinds of initiatives can provide impetus to consider wider reform agendas and different regulatory instruments, which recognise and harness the innovations made in scholarship around new forms used by government to affect the behaviour of more powerful agents.

Integrate local and global structures

In their groundbreaking analysis of *Global business regulation*, Braithwaite and Drahos (2000) considered the actions of a range of agents. First, there were states and international organisations of states in the form of intergovernmental economic and social institutions, 'actors' as they call them. Other actors include business organisations and NGOs, whose regulatory roles typically include policy implementation, especially in the role of public service providers. Provision, distribution and regulation must intermingle in the minds of regulators. Braithwaite and Drahos' regulatory 'principles' and 'mechanisms' also take in key coordination as well as regulatory functions, and most often trans-national coordination at that. Their principles include concepts of 'world's best practice' and their mechanisms include 'non-reciprocal coordination'. These are key ingredients of the argument of this chapter, that there must be reconciliation in regulation between international market competition and trans-national cooperation.

This is made easier, if, as Krahmann (2003) argues, regulation (although she uses governance) is conceived as one phenomenon equally applicable to analysis of the global, regional and national levels, rather than being many and varied concepts. This does not mean that the connections are there, or that regulation applies in the same ways at all levels. Rather, the point is that Braithwaite and Drahos' actors, principles and mechanisms are themselves equally applicable, and scholarship may benefit from integrating consideration of them at various geographic levels. This is consistent with an emergent tradition in regulation, governance, policy and international relations scholarship (see, for example, Sassen, 2002a, 2007a, 2007b; Gough, 2004; Larner and Walters, 2004; Slaughter, 2004; Swyngedouw, 2004, 2005). The welfare and citizenship dimensions of the same tradition lie in the previously discussed literature on global social policy, and most directly Deacon's (2007) concept of 'global social regulation'.

Casting aside the conceptual confusions between regulation and governance, and using both concepts, it emerged from our interviews that there must be more effective coordination between the local and global levels of regulation. This means that there should be rules and norms that formally align national governments with international rule- and law-making institutions such as the WTO and UNESCO. In international education, while acknowledging the shortcomings of the theory and the contemporary practice of free trade, a greater role for the WTO is implied in extending the principle of the level playing field in the trade of international education between nations. Trade lawyers and international economists need to negotiate with national legislators and university officials on the terms on which such formal regulations may turn. This may help to ease pressure on exporter nations to compete by means of marketing without social responsibility, and thereby reduce the tendency towards some of the negative experiences of students that this analysis has identified. That is, the incentives to treat market expansion as the primary motivation will be downgraded.

Conclusion: students as trans-national citizenship subjects in practice

The integration of global and local services is not out of step in principle with longstanding suggestions by social democratic scholars to move the governance of world affairs from a neoliberal to a more cosmopolitan regulatory basis. As Archibugi and Held (1995b) identified in the mid-1990s, for example, post-Cold War politics increasingly called for the protection of the rights of minorities, but such protection had to be more trans-national in structure. Protection, they argued, was increasingly a matter for the world community as a whole. Cosmopolitanism was important in that it indicated a trans-national organisational model – although it went further in terms of the integration inherent to the process of globalisation – 'in which citizens, wherever they are located in the world, have a voice, input and political representation in international affairs, in parallel with and independently of their own governments' (Archibugi and Held, 1995a, p 5). Our analysis suggests that governments and international institutions need to reconstruct international students as citizens along similar lines. This would change the basis of both international education marketing and the services and protections offered international students, although this runs counter to the current patterns of treating them as fee-paying trans-national education consumers. Students' status as legal citizens of their home country and non-citizens of the host country needs to be rethought. While full social citizenship in the host country is not proposed, a reconstruction of international student rights is needed.

The many and complex challenges inherent to the application of trans-national citizenship should not and cannot be discounted (see especially Hudson and Slaughter, 2007). Part of the challenge here is to coordinate the support structures. As McBurnie and Ziguras (2001) argue in their analysis of TNHE in three Southeast Asian countries, regulation varies according to the central rationale of the national regime. Despite such variations, governments have the capacity to embed international education within common agendas that should be trans-national; that is, social citizenship agendas with trans-national principles and the trans-national experiences of students in mind. Scholars of international education regulation could subject these agendas to greater scrutiny in fulfilling part of their role in trans-national understandings of citizenship.

Even if international students are to be viewed as market subjects to the exclusion of citizenship, both universities and national economies may lose 'customers' if their treatment of students is perceived internationally as sub-standard. We have discussed in earlier chapters examples of this in both Australia and New Zealand. This argument has long been recognised in popular and scholarly sources alike (see, for example, Mazzarol and Soutar, 2002; Deumert et al, 2005), and in legal institutions. As we have argued, not only are most market participants deserving of protection from the market's excesses, but in Polanyi's (1944) methodology, the market mechanism itself could not be reproduced without all classes (including, in his words, the 'trading' and 'landed classes') being adequately covered by socially protective institutions. Consistent with this, as argued by the Deputy President of the Australian Administrative Appeals Tribunal, using Section 29 of the ESOS Act in a case involving student fee refunds by an education provider (cited in Jackson, 2004, pp 360-1): 'to safeguard the ongoing income from this source [cross-border education] … it is necessary to have a regulatory framework in place to ensure the quality of the educational services provided and to protect student funds.' Our argument is that this kind of logic is a good starting point, although it should apply not just to the protection of funds, but to the protection and advancement of people.

Note

[1] Here, given that in education studies the term 'institution' often refers to universities, colleges and schools, in order to avoid confusion the term 'support structures' is used in place of institutions. In that sense we depart from common practice in the non-education social sciences (see especially Thelen and Steinmo, 1992).

NINE

Conclusion

Managing global mobility

In international education, the language that appears in formal regulation does not reflect the student experience on the ground. Given the evidence uncovered through interview data with students and service and policy staff, the Australian regime is not entirely true to the promise of the ESOS Framework to provide 'student welfare and support services' and 'nationally consistent standards for dealing with student complaints and appeals' (DEST, 2007b, Part A.3.1). The New Zealand Pastoral Care Code comes closer than Australia to fulfilling its stated *raison d'être*: 'to provide a framework for education providers for the pastoral care of international students' (MOENZ, 2011a, p 2). Yet New Zealand's Code does not deliver 'welfare' (Part 5) as reasonably defined by social scientists, and although the Code does provide for nationally consistent 'grievance procedures' (Part 7), this is not achieved for enough students who simultaneously know about it and need it.

In both Australia and New Zealand the necessary flow of regulatory information to students is deficient. The analyst who digs beneath the surface of the formal regulatory rhetoric is led to look for the unofficial and less explored ways in which students seek to augment their own welfare. Regulation theory helps in the process of determining how everyday experiences are shaped by forces that are not obvious to the untrained eye. Theory also assists in examining what lies beyond the informal arrangements that students make in the context of a system that our analysis has found to be overly reliant on the global market forces that govern international education. The problem we set out to investigate has led to a conceptual lens which is not common in the field of international education. It produces the conclusion that Australia and New Zealand both use formal regulation to service the competition state strategy that they pursue with equal vigour.

Signature contributions to regulation theory in recent years emphasise several key concepts discussed in this book, but these start form one central point: that the traditional understanding of regulation as a top-down process using command and control – and as deriving directly from the state to the citizen – falls short of explaining how individuals, societies and economies are affected by regulation. This is the case not least because international students are not constructed as citizens by systems of regulation in either the formal or informal senses; and once they migrate temporarily for their studies, neither do they keep all of their citizenship rights in the home country. Our interrogation of how the lives of international students are affected by regulation backs up the need to explore regulation in all of its forms.

Where the formal sphere falls short, typically students seek out the support of family, friendship and social networks. Some of these are trans-national in scope and coverage. Yet the networks do not fully compensate, with students in Australia and New Zealand reporting high levels of isolation, loneliness and the need for greater induction into the host country culture. Service provider interviewees concurred intuitively, drawing on their experience of attending to problems. This intuition was less likely to be shared by staff engaged in policy. Support structures include the student self (Marginson et al, 2010, Chapter 15), with self-regulation being a common and necessary feature. Staff interviewees in the policy sphere tended to argue that this was as it should be. However, although it may seem fair enough for students to be independent and for formal regulation to encourage generalised self-reliance, to infer that existing formal support structures are adequate, as some did, is not wholly reasonable. Attention should be devoted in particular to the gaps between the protections enjoyed by local students and their international counterparts. Moral questions need to be posed as to the appropriateness of such gaps and decisions made about which spheres of wellbeing and which kinds of services might be the same for students in both categories.

Consistent with the premise and the cautions of regulation theorists (Black, 2002; Parker et al, 2004; Arup et al, 2006), we have also suggested that the role of law be rethought in light of the relationship between formal and informal regulation. Law can be feeble and incomplete unless considered alongside non-law variables such as 'policy, markets and civil society institutions' (Carney et al, 2006, p 383). In addition and alongside the nexus between law and non-law protections, national regulations, whether top-down or more decentralised, formal or informal, are affected by trans-national and global regulatory structures. In this space are IGOs and global civil society. As argued in Chapter Eight, the converse is also true, and there is a two-way relationship between global and local, particularly as regards questions of student rights and the determination of citizenship. Analytically this backs the need for interdisciplinary mindsets to understand the web of decentralised, multilateral relations of regulation.

Reinforcing the work of authors such as Ayres and Braithwaite (1992; see also Braithwaite, 2006, 2008), although it may be constructed politically as forward-looking or proactive, formal regulation can be adaptive to negative or positive circumstances and developments. Otherwise stated, regulation can be as much responsive and pragmatic as strategic and visionary. As discussed in Chapter Five, in the case of Australia in recent years there have been significant diplomatic efforts on the part of authorities to dispel perceptions that Indian students are in danger if they choose to study in Australia. As outlined in Chapter Five, a year before the final writing of this book there was a sharp downturn in the number of incoming Indian students. As part of the diplomatic agenda, Australian representatives at both state and federal levels travelled to India for talks, and Indian dignitaries travelled to Australia. As also mentioned in Chapter Six, in New Zealand some seven years earlier than the current downturn, anti-Chinese and generally anti-Asian student sentiments were evident in sections of the wider society, and the Pastoral Care Code can be seen partly as a means to address racial and other forms of discrimination. Both Australia and New Zealand's frameworks also reacted to instances of the need to set up fee insurance for students in the case of educational institutions not being able, for whatever reason, to deliver the courses they were obliged to provide. In short, in both countries the Codes were clear cases of responsive regulation.

Yet international education scholarship has arguably not caught up with the need for perspectives on regulation beyond traditional top-down command and control. The urgency of informal protections initiated and serviced by students themselves, and their networks, has thus far been all but invisible. Our analysis contributes to filling the gap in relation to the impact of regulation on student welfare, although it is open to further adaptation in other areas relevant to cross-border and trans-national education, such as quality control, the education–migration nexus, and distance and other virtual and physical-presence projects.

Perhaps the key underlying perspective is that of political economy, which begins from the proposition that markets do not function in isolation, in the process addressing 'the connections between economic problems, social structures, and political processes' (Stilwell, 2006, p 10). The key driving force in regulation – at least the nation-state portion as discussed here – is the market and the search by nations for competitive advantage. This occurs within various policy and regulatory contexts. The state is a competition state, and Australia and New Zealand are cases in point. This was made clear in Chapters Three and Four in the context of the discussion of the global market and the place of these two key exporter countries within it. It was also substantiated in Chapters Five and Six in the in-depth discussions of each national regime. We come to the conclusion that international competition is central, having found slightly different motivations between the two countries. Australia's approach is driven by competition less via welfare than through consumer protection and compliance by education institutions. New Zealand's approach seems more comprehensive, embracing pastoral care. On paper that is superior, but it does not foster wellbeing. New Zealand regulation is arguably driven by a combination of pastoral care language and a consumer protection approach in practice, with institution compliance also a key feature, much as is the case in Australia.

Summary, argument and concluding remarks

Moving toward a regulatory regime that fits the criteria put forward in summary form in Chapter Eight, and discussed at greater length throughout this book, requires a process of managing the welfare of globally mobile individuals. International students travel between countries, and many traverse the seas and continents from one end of the world to the other in pursuit of education. Thus far, in countries such as those of central interest here, namely, Australia and New Zealand, it is mainly, although not exclusively, the market forces of supply and demand that regulate students' overseas experiences.

Australia and New Zealand typify the market approach. Both have extensive codification in formal regulatory programmes, incorporating quality assurance, migration provisions, campus-based laws and national legislation (and state-level laws in Australia), and elaborate regimes governing the social and administrative rights of students. Our comparative analysis found that there were significant differences between the two in terms of the substance and language employed in formal regulation between Australia's ESOS Framework and New Zealand's Pastoral Care Code. However, we argue that formal regulation in international education is less important than the informal dimension, and the latter is most important when when formal regulation is most deficient. Formal and informal sources of welfare are not mutually reinforcing, and neither does one compensate for the other. Their combination is always somewhat unpredictable and in need of progressive social engineering. Markets, after all, do not naturally cater evenly or equitably for human wellbeing.

Building on the comparative analysis and an overriding theoretical analysis of international education regulation, we have argued that international student wellbeing relies on national and trans-national regulation. Consistent with this, the conceptual map summarising our conclusions guides us towards a four-way relationship, between formal national, informal national, formal trans-national and informal trans-national forms of welfare. That necessarily calls on students to use their agency to self-regulate and partly to look after their own welfare, which is ethically appropriate given that no individual in society is or should be 100 per cent reliant on publicly provided safety nets. However, we see more of a role for formal regulation in managing the student wellbeing question.

Finally, on writing this book we have come to an important theoretical reflection, a conclusion of sorts but certainly not one which ends with the current analysis. Regulation theory is tremendously useful in providing a conceptual language for understanding international student wellbeing. This is, of course, not to dismiss analyses of the same issues through non-regulatory frameworks and concepts. In international education, as in many spheres of human welfare, regulation is not everything and it is certainly not suitable for every context. Our finding that Australia and New Zealand are empirically similar while also being different in formal regulation serves as both a vindication of regulatory theory and a critique of it. While on the former proposition regulation adherents may argue that the concept of informal regulation saves the day – and their theoretical perspective – on the latter one may ask, as we did on the basis of our comparative analysis, does regulation matter? Our suggestion is that it can matter, but it does not seem to be as consequential as it should be in international education. To delve further into this question we invite comparative regulation scholars who examine other countries to enter the debate.

In the absence of evidence from these other countries, given that few comprehensive analyses are yet to enter the literature, our own practical conclusions for reform stand as outlined in Chapter Eight. First, international students themselves must be conceived as the first logical layer or source of their own welfare. The second is students' local, national and trans-national family, friendship and social networks. This includes campus-based and other NGOs, some of which can be faith-based, and local community networks in general. More formal sources are important. Hence our third layer consists of local and national support structures in the host country, including migration and education ministries and also the police and other emergency services, health and transport services and the like. Above the national level are the intergovernmental organisations such as UN agencies and the WTO, and international NGOs and representative bodies.

Beyond the practical level are the more strategic and big-picture concepts that we suggest can guide reform towards simultaneous consideration of the local, national and global arenas. Regulatory authorities and policy makers must also be able to conceive of the relationship between regulation and governance, and apply such understandings to the national and trans-national levels. At the national level governments need to conceptualise and apply understandings of consultative democracy and whole-of-government initiatives to international education, especially given that, as we have found, students' lives are affected by more policy spheres than just education and migration. In short, national support structures and services need to be better planned and more effectively delivered. Finally, and perhaps most importantly, international students must be treated, formally in policy but also informally, as subjects of trans-national citizenship. In the end, a combination of scholarship and practical action is needed to design and to install that citizenship.

References

ABS (Australian Bureau of Statistics) (2011) 'International trade in services by country, by state and by detailed services category, financial year 2009-10', Canberra: ABS (www.abs.gov.au/ausstats/abs@.nsf/PrimaryMainFeatures/5368.0.55.003).

AEI (Australian Education International) (2007) 'ESOS National Code' (www.aei.gov.au/Regulatory-Information/Education-Services-for-overseas-students-esos-legislative-framework/national-code/Pages/default.aspx).

AEI (2011) 'ESOS easy guide' (www.aei.gov.au/Regulatory-Information/Education-Services-for-Overseas-Students-ESOS-Legislative-Framework/ESOSQuickInformation/ESOSEasyGuide/Pages/ESOSEasyGuide.aspx).

AEI (2012) 'International student enrolments in Australia 1994-2011' (https://aei.gov.au/research/International-Student-Data/Documents/INTERNATIONAL%20STUDENT%20DATA/2011/2011%20Time%20Series%20Graph.pdf).

AFIS (Australian Federation of International Students) (2011) www.internationalstudents.org.au/

AHRC (Australian Human Rights Commission) (2009) 'Communiqué: Human rights of international students a major issue', Sydney: AHRC (www.hreoc.gov.au/about/media/media_releases/2009/107_09.html).

AHRC (2011) 'Information for students: What are human rights and why are they important?', Sydney: AHRC (www.hreoc.gov.au/info_for_students/).

Alford, J. (2008) 'The limits to traditional public administration, or rescuing public value from misrepresentation', *Australian Journal of Public Administration*, vol 67, no 3, pp 357-66.

Altbach, P.G. (2007) *Tradition and transition: The international imperative in higher education*, Rotterdam/Boston, MA: Sense Publishers/Center for International Higher Education, Boston College.

Angus, L. (2004) 'Globalisation and educational change: Bringing about the reshaping and reforming of practice', *Journal of Education Policy*, vol 19, no 1, pp 23-41.

Apple, M.W., Kenway, J. and Singh, M. (eds) (2005) *Globalizing education: Policies, pedagogies, and politics*, New York: Peter Lang.

AQF (Australian Qualifications Framework) (2010) 'The Australian Qualifications Framework', Adelaide: AQF Council (www.aqf.edu.au/AbouttheAQF/TheAQF/tabid/108/Default.aspx).

Archibugi, D. and Held, D. (1995a) 'Editors' introduction', in D. Archibugi and D. Held (eds) *Cosmopolitan democracy: An agenda for a new world order*, Cambridge: Polity Press, pp 1-16.

Archibugi, D. and Held, D. (eds) (1995b) *Cosmopolitan democracy: An agenda for a new world order*, Cambridge: Polity Press.

Archives New Zealand (2011) *Education*, Wellington: Archives New Zealand (http://archives.govt.nz/research/guides/education).

Arup, C., Gahan, P., Howe, J., Johnstone, R., Mitchell, R. and O'Donnell, A. (eds) (2006) *Labour law and labour market regulation: Essays on the construction, constitution and regulation of labour markets and work relationships*, Leichhardt, NSW: Federation Press.

Astor, H. (2005) 'Improving dispute resolution in Australian universities: Options for the future', *Journal of Higher Education and Management*, vol 27, no 1, pp 49-65.

AUQA (Australian Universities Quality Agency) (2010) 'Mission, objectives, vision and values', Melbourne: AUQA (http://www.teqsa. gov.au/about-teqsa).

Australian Government (2008) *Review of Australian higher education*, Canberra: Department of Education, Employment and Workplace Relations.

Australian Government (2009) *Welfare of International Students, Report of the parliamentary Senate Standing Committee*, Canberra: Commonwealth of Australia.

Australian Government (2010) *Stronger, simpler, smarter ESOS: Supporting international students – Review of the Education Services for Overseas Students (ESOS) Act 2000*, Canberra: Commonwealth of Australia.

Ayres, I. and Braithwaite, J. (1992) *Responsive regulation: Transcending the deregulation debate*, New York: Oxford University Press.

Baas, M. (2007) 'The language of migration: The education industry versus the migration industry', *People and Place*, vol 15, no 2, pp 49-60.

Baird, B. (2009) 'Review of the Education Services for Overseas Students (ESOS) Act 2000', Issues Paper, Canberra: Commonwealth of Australia.

Baldwin, R. and Cave, M. (1999) *Understanding regulation: Theory, strategy, and practice*, Oxford: Oxford University Press.

Baldwin, R., Scott, C. and Hood, C. (eds) (1998) *A reader on regulation*, Oxford: Oxford University Press.

Barrie, S.M. (2006) 'Understanding what we mean by the generic attributes of graduates', *Higher Education*, vol 51, no 2, pp 215-41.

Bashir, S. (2007) *Trends in international trade in higher education: Implications and options for developing countries*, Education Working Paper Series 6, Washington: The World Bank.

Begg, D. (2008) 'Banks to blame for financial crisis', Dublin: Irish Congress of Trade Unions (www.ictu.ie/press/2008/10/03/banks-to-blame-for-financial-crisis/).

Bennett, J. (2011) 'Bowen says student visa program unsustainable', *Campus Review*, 14 June, p 4.

Bergan, S. (2004) 'A tale of two cultures in higher education policies: The rule of law or an excess of legalism?', *Journal of Studies in International Education*, vol 8, no 2, pp 172-85.

Birrell, R.J. (2009) 'Immigration policy change and the international student industry', *People and Place*, vol 17, no 2, pp 64-80.

Birrell, R.J. and Smith, F. (2010) 'Export earnings from the overseas student industry: how much?', *Australian Universities Review*, vol 52, no 1, pp 4-12.

Bitzer, E. (2002) 'South African legislation on limiting private and foreign higher education: Protecting the public or ignoring globalisation?', *South African Journal of Higher Education*, vol 16, no 1, pp 22-8.

Black, J. (2001) 'Managing discretion', Paper presented at Conference on 'Penalties: Policy, Principles and Practice in Government Regulation', Darling Harbour, Sydney, 7-9 June.

Black, J. (2002) 'Critical reflections on regulation', *Australian Journal of Legal Philosophy*, vol 27, pp 1-37.

Black, J. (2003) 'Enrolling actors in regulatory systems: examples from UK financial services regulation', *Public Law*, Spring, pp 63-91.

Block, F. and Somers, M.R. (1984) 'Beyond the economistic fallacy: The holistic social science of Karl Polanyi', in T. Skocpol (ed) *Vision and method in historical sociology*, Cambridge: Cambridge University Press, pp 47-84.

Bond, S., Areepattamannil, S., Braithwaite-Sturgeon, G., Hayle, E. and Malekan, M. (2007) *Northern lights: International graduates of Canadian institutions and the national workforce*, Ottawa: Canadian Bureau for International Education.

Braithwaite, J. (2006) 'Responsive regulation and developing economies', *World Development*, vol 35, no 5, pp 884-98.

Braithwaite, J. (2008) *Regulatory capitalism: How it works, ideas for making it work better*, Cheltenham, UK/Northampton, MA: Edward Elgar.

Braithwaite, J. and Drahos, P. (2000) *Global business regulation*, Cambridge: Cambridge University Press.

Braithwaite, J., Levi-Faur, D. and Coglianese, C. (2007) 'Can regulation and governance make a difference?', *Regulation and Governance*, vol 1, no 1, pp 1-7.

Bray, M. and Haworth, N. (eds) (1993) *Economic restructuring and industrial relations in Australia and New Zealand: A comparative analysis*, Australian Centre for Industrial Relations Research and Teaching (ACIRRT) Monograph No 8, Sydney, NSW: ACIRRT, University of Sydney.

Bugra, A. and Agartan, K. (2007) *Reading Karl Polanyi for the twenty-first century: Market economy as a political project*, Basingstoke: Palgrave Macmillan.

Butcher, A. (2003), 'Whither international students? The absence of international student policy during New Zealand's university reforms from 1984 to 1999', *New Zealand Journal of Educational Studies*, vol 38, no 2, pp 151-64.

Butcher, A. and McGrath, T. (2004) 'International students in New Zealand: Needs and responses', *International Education Journal*, vol 5, no 4, pp 540-51.

CAPA (Council of Australian Postgraduate Associations Incorporated) (2011) 'Issues', Melbourne, VIC: CAPA (www.capa.edu.au/issues).

Caramani, D. (2010) 'Of differences and similarities: Is the explanation of variation a limitation to (or of) comparative analysis?', *European Political Science*, vol 9, no 1, pp 34-48.

Carney, T., Ramia, G., and Chapman, A. (2006) 'Which law is the laggard? Regulation and the gaps between labour law and social security law', in C. Arup, P. Gahan, J. Howe, R. Johnstone, R. Mitchell and A. O'Donnell (eds) *Labour law and labour market regulation: Essays on the construction, constitution and regulation of labour markets and work relationships*, Sydney: Federation Press, pp 383-409.

Castles, F.G. (1985) *The working class and welfare: Reflections on the political development of the welfare state in Australia and New Zealand, 1890-1980*, Wellington: Allen & Unwin/Port Nicholson Press.

Castles, F.G. (1988) *Australian public policy and economic vulnerability: A comparative and historical perspective*, Sydney: Allen & Unwin.

Castles, F.G. (1989) 'Social protection by other means: Australia's strategy of coping with external vulnerability', in F.G. Castles (ed) *The comparative history of public policy*, Oxford: Oxford University Press, pp 16-55.

Castles, F.G. (1992) 'On sickness days and social policy', *Australian and New Zealand Journal of Sociology*, vol 28, no 1, pp 29-43.

Castles, F.G. (1994) 'The wage earners' welfare state revisited: Refurbishing the established model of Australian social protection, 1983-93', *Australian Journal of Social Issues*, vol 29, no 2, pp 120-45.

Castles, F.G. (1996) 'Needs-based strategies of social protection in Australia and New Zealand', in G. Esping-Andersen (ed) *Welfare states in transition: National adaptations in global economies*, London: Sage Publications, pp 88-115.

Castles, F.G. (1997) 'Historical and comparative perspectives on the Australian welfare state: A response to Watts', *Australian and New Zealand Journal of Sociology*, vol 33, no 1, pp 16-20.

Castles, F.G. and Pierson, C. (1996) 'A new convergence? Recent policy developments in the United Kingdom, Australia and New Zealand', *Policy & Politics*, vol 24, no 3, pp 233-46.

Castles, F.G., Vowles, J. and Gerritsen, R. (eds) (1996) *The great experiment: Labour parties and public policy transformation in Australia and New Zealand*, Sydney: Allen & Unwin.

Cerny, P. (1997) 'Paradoxes of the competition state: The dynamics of political globalisation', *Government and Opposition*, vol 32, no 2, pp 251-74.

Cholewinski, R. (1997) *Migrant workers in international human rights law: Their protection in countries of employment*, Oxford: Clarendon Press.

COAG (Council of Australian Governments) (2009) 'Communiqué: Council of Australian Governments Meeting', 2 July (http://www.coag.gov.au/node/66#5.%20International%20Students%20Strategy).

Collins, F. (2006) 'Making Asian students, making students Asian: The racialisation of export education in Auckland, New Zealand', *Asia Pacific Viewpoint*, vol 47, no 2, pp 217-34.

CPAG (Child Poverty Action Group) (2008) *Welfare benefits and tax credits handbook* (10th edn), London: CPAG.

Daniel, J.S. (2002) 'Quality assurance, accreditation and recognition of qualifications in higher education in an international perspective', in IAU (International Association of Universities), *Globalisation and the market in higher education*, Paris: UNESCO (United Nations Educational, Scientific and Cultural Organisation)/IAU, pp 11-19.

Davis, G. (2010) *The republic of learning: Higher education transforms Australia,* Sydney: HarperCollins Publishers.

Dawkins, K. (2003) *Global governance: The battle over planetary power,* New York: Seven Stories Press.

Deacon, B. (2007) *Global social policy and governance*, London: Sage Publications.

Deacon, B. with Hulse, M. and Stubs, P. (1997) *Global social policy: International organisations and the future of welfare*, London: Sage Publications.

DEEWR (Department of Education, Employment and Workplace Relations) (2011) *Selected higher education statistics*, Canberra, ACT: DEEWR (www.deewr.gov.au/HigherEducation/Publications/HEStatistics/Publications/Pages/Home.aspx).

Deloitte Access Economics (2011) *Broader implications from a downturn in international students*, Report for Universities Australia, Canberra: Universities Australia.

DEST (Department of Education, Science and Training) (2007a) *Education Services for Overseas Students Act 2000*, Canberra: Office of Legal Drafting, Attorney-General's Department.

DEST (2007b) *National code of practice for registration authorities and training to overseas students*, Canberra: J.S. McMillan Printing Group.

DEST (2007c) 'Standard 6 – student support services', Australian Education International https://www.aei.gov.au/Regulatory-Information/Education-Services-for-Overseas-Students-ESOS-Legislative-Framework/National-Code/nationalcodepartd/Pages/ExplanatoryguideD6.aspx).

Deumert, A., Marginson, S., Nyland, C., Ramia, G. and Sawir, E. (2005) 'Migration and social protection rights: The social and economic security of cross-border students in Australia', *Global Social Policy*, vol 5, no 3, pp 329-52.

Douglass, J., Edelstein, R. and Hoaraeu, C. (2011) 'US: Where do international students choose to study?', *University World News*, no 166, 10 April.

Drahos, P. and Braithwaite, J. (2001) 'The globalisation of regulation', *Journal of Political Philosophy*, vol 9, no 1, pp 103-28.

Enders, J. (2004) 'Higher education, internationalisation, and the nation-state: recent developments and challenges in governance theory', *Higher Education*, vol 47, no 3, pp 361-82.

ENZ (2011) 'Statistics', Wellington: ENZ (http://educationnz.govt.nz/strategyresearchstats/statistics).

Farrington, D.J. and Palfreyman, D. (2006) *The law of higher education*, Oxford: Oxford University Press.

FISA (Federation of Indian Students Incorporated) (2011) 'Integrating, representing and empowering Indian students in Australia' (https://www.facebook.com/fisa.aus).

Fordham, M. (2006) 'Comparative legal traditions – Introducing the common law to civil lawyers in Asia', *Asian Journal of Comparative Law*, vol 1, no 1, pp 1-8.

Foucault, M. (1977-78/2007) *Security, territory, population: Lectures at the Collège de France* (edited by M. Senellart), New York/Basingstoke: Palgrave Macmillan.

Fox, J. (2005) 'Unpacking "transnational citizenship"', *Annual Review of Political Science*, vol 8, pp 171-201.

Frederickson, H.G. (2005) 'Whatever happened to public administration? Governance, governance everywhere', in E. Ferlie, L.E. Lyn and C. Pollitt (eds) *The Oxford handbook of public management*, Oxford: Oxford University Press, pp 282-304.

Geddes, B. (2003) *Paradigms and sand castles: Theory building and research design in comparative politics*, Ann Arbor, MI: The University of Michigan Press.

Gilbert, N. (2002) *Transformation of the welfare state: The silent surrender of public responsibility*, Oxford: Oxford University Press.

Goddard, B. (2011) 'Future perspectives: Horizon 2025', Unpublished manuscript.

Goodin, R.E. (ed) (1996) *The theory of institutional design*, Cambridge: Cambridge University Press.

Gough, I. (2004) 'Human well-being and social structures: Relating the universal and the local', *Global Social Policy*, vol 4, no 3, pp 289-311.

Graycar, A. (2010) *Racism and the tertiary student experience in Australia*, Occasional Paper 5/10, Canberra: Academy of the Social Sciences in Australia.

Green, M. and Ferguson, A. (2011) *Internationalisation of US higher education in a time of declining resources*, Report commissioned by Australian Education International (AEI), Canberra: AEI.

Halliday, F. (2008) 'The revenge of ideas: Karl Polanyi and Susan Strange', London: Open Democracy (www.opendemocracy.net/article/the-revenge-of-ideas-karl-polanyi-and-susan-strange).

Hansen, R. (2009) 'The poverty of postnationalism: Citizenship, immigration, and the New Europe', *Theory and Society*, vol 38, no 1, pp 1-24.

Hare, J. (2010) 'Coming together', *Campus Review*, vol 21, no 14, p 1.

Harris, N. (2007) 'Resolution of student complaints in higher education institutions', *Legal Studies*, vol 27, no 4, pp 566-603.

Harvey, M., Ramlogan, R. and Randles, S. (2007) *Karl Polanyi: New perspectives on the place of the economy in society*, Manchester: Manchester University Press.

Held, D. (1995) *Democracy and the global order: From the modern state to cosmopolitan governance*, Cambridge: Polity Press.

Held, D. (2004) *Global covenant: The social democratic alternative to the Washington consensus*, Cambridge: Polity Press.

Held, D. and McGrew, A. (2000) 'The great globalisation debate: An introduction', in D. Held, and A. McGrew (eds) *The global transformations reader: An introduction to the globalisation debate*, Cambridge: Polity Press, pp 1-46.

Hira, A. (2003) 'The brave new world of international education', *World Economy*, vol 26, no 6, pp 911-31.

Hodson, P.J. and Thomas, H.G. (2001) 'Higher education as an international commodity: Ensuring quality in partnerships', *Assessment and Evaluation in Higher Education*, vol 26, no 2, pp 101-12.

Hudson, W. and Slaughter, S. (eds) (2007) *Globalisation and citizenship: The transnational challenge*, London/New York: Routledge.

IAU (International Association of Universities) (2002) *Globalisation and the market in higher education*, Paris: UNESCO (United Nations Educational, Scientific and Cultural Organisation)/IAU.

IIE (Institute of International Education) (2011) *Data on US foreign students*, New York: IIE (www.iie.org/en/Research-and-Publications/Open-Doors.aspx).

IOM (International Organization for Migration) (2008) *World migration report 2008: Managing labour mobility in the evolving global economy*, Geneva: IOM.

IOM (2011) (http://www.iom.int/cms/en/sites/iom/home/about-iom-1/mission.html).

ISM (International Student Movement) (2009a) 'What is the ISM?', ISM (http://ism-global.net/ism_en).

ISM (2009b) 'International joint statement', ISM (http://ism-global.net/international_joint_statement).

ISM (2013) 'International Student Movement - A Communication Platform', ISM Facebook page: at: http://www.facebook.com/notes/international-student-movement/international-student-movement-ism-a-communication-platform/180748141967692

Iversen, T. (1996) 'Power, flexibility, and the breakdown of centralized wage bargaining: Denmark and Sweden in comparative perspective', *Comparative Politics*, vol 28, no 4, pp 399-436.

Jackson, J. (2004) 'Regulation of international education: Australia and New Zealand', Paper presented at Australia and New Zealand Education Law Association Conference, Wellington.

Jackson, J. (2005) 'Regulation of international education: Australia and New Zealand', *Australia & New Zealand Journal of Law and Education*, vol 10/11, no 1, pp 67-82.

Jackson, J. and Varnham, S. (2007) *Law for educators: School and university law in Australia*, Chatswood, NSW: LexisNexis Butterworths.

Jackson, J., Fleming, H., Kamvounias, P. and Varnham, S. (2009) *Student grievances and discipline matters project*, Sydney, NSW: Australian Learning and Teaching Council.

Jakubowicz, A. with Monani, D. (2010) *International student futures in Australia: A human rights perspective on moving forward to real action*, Occasional Paper 6/2010, Canberra: Academy of the Social Sciences in Australia.

Jobbins, D. (2011) 'UK: Government eases crackdown on student visas', *University World News*, vol 164, 27 March.

Kaplan, W.A. and Lee, B.A. (2006) *The law of higher education: A comprehensive guide to legal implications of administrative decision making* (4th edn), Volumes I and II, San Francisco, CA: Jossey-Bass.

Katzenstein, P.J. (2003) 'Small states and small states revisited', *New Political Economy*, vol 8, no 1, pp 9-30.

Kelsey, J. (1993) *Rolling back the state: Privatisation of power in Aotearoa/ New Zealand*, Wellington: Bridget Williams Books.

Kelsey, J. (1995) *Economic fundamentalism: The New Zealand experiment – A world model for structural adjustment?*, London: Pluto Press.

King, A. and Scheider, B. (1991) *The first global revolution: A report of the council of Rome*, New York: Pantheon.

Kleingeld, P. (1998) 'Kant's cosmopolitan law: World citizenship for a global order', *Kantian Review*, vol 2, pp 72-90.

Knight, J. (2004) 'Crossborder education in a trade environment: Complexities and policy implications', Paper delivered to Workshop on Implications of WTO (World Trade Organization)/GATS (General Agreement on Trade in Services) or Higher Education in Africa, African Association of Universities, Accra Ghana, 27-29 April.

Knight, M. (2011) *Strategic review of the student visa program 2011*, Canberra: Australian Government (www.immi.gov.au/students/_pdf/2011-knight-review.pdf).

Krahmann, E. (2003) 'National, regional, and global governance: One phenomenon or many?', *Global Governance*, vol 9, no 3, pp 323-46.

Larner, W. and Walters, W. (2004) *Global governmentality: Governing international spaces*, London: Routledge.

Le Grand, J. and Bartlett, W. (1993) *Quasi-markets and social policy*, London: Macmillan.

Lewis, N. (2005) 'Code of practice for the pastoral care of international students: Making a globalising industry in New Zealand', *Globalisation, Societies and Education*, vol 3, no 1, pp 5-47.

Li, M. (2007) 'The impact of the media on the New Zealand export education industry', Paper presented at the Inaugural Australia-China International Business Research Conference, Beijing, China, 22-24 September.

Lim, P.H. and Hyatt, J. (2009) 'Educational accountability – Do tertiary students need more academic protection in New Zealand', *International Journal of Law and Education*, vol 14, no 1, pp 23-38.

Lloyd, D. (1981) *The idea of law*, Harmondsworth: Penguin Books.

MAC (Management Advisory Committee) (2004) *Connecting government: Whole of government responses to Australia's priority challenges*, Canberra: Commonwealth of Australia.

McBurnie, G. and Ziguras, C. (2001) 'The regulation of transnational higher education in southeast Asia: Case studies of Hong Kong, Malaysia and Australia', *Higher Education*, vol 42, no 1, pp 85-105.

McBurnie, G. and Ziguras, C. (2006) *Transnational education: Issues and trends in offshore higher education*, London: Routledge.

McBurnie, G. and Ziguras, C. (2007) 'Institutions, not students, get the travel bug', *Far Eastern Economic Review*, vol 170, no 1, pp 58-61.

McGrath, T., Beaven, S., Chong, J. and Eriquez, R. (2008) 'Connecting international students, domestic students and community people in campus, classroom and community situations', Paper presented to the 19th ISANA (International Student Advisers Network of Australia Inc) (Australia and New Zealand) International Education Conference, Auckland, 2-5 December.

McKenzie-McLean, J. (2007) '"Crazed animals" in racist attack', *The Press*, 2 August, p 1.

Mahoney, J., Kimball, E. and Koivu, K.L. (2009) 'The logic of historical explanation in the social sciences', *Comparative Political Studies*, vol 42, no 1, pp 114-46.

Marginson, S. (2004) 'Competition and markets in higher education: A "glonacal" analysis', *Policy Futures in Higher Education*, vol 2, no 2, pp 175-244.

Marginson, S. (2005) 'Dynamics of national and global competition in higher education', *Higher Education*, vol 52, no 1, pp 1-39.

Marginson, S. (2011) 'Imagining the global', in R. King, S. Marginson and R. Naidoo (eds) *Handbook of higher education and globalisation*, Cheltenham: Edward Elgar, pp 10-39.

Marginson, S. (2012) 'Including the other: Regulation of the human rights of mobile students in a nation-bound world', *Higher Education*. vol 63, no 4, pp 497-512.

Marginson, S. and Considine, M. (2000) *The enterprise university,* Cambridge: Cambridge University Press.

Marginson, S. and Mollis, M. (2000) 'Comparing national education systems in the global era', *Australian Universities Review*, vol 42, no 2, pp 53-63.

Marginson, S. and Rhoades, G. (2002) 'Beyond national states, markets, and systems of higher education: A glonacal agency heuristic', *Higher Education*, vol 43, no 3, pp 281-309.

Marginson, S., Nyland, C., Sawir, E. and Forbes-Mewett, H. (2010) *International student security*, Cambridge, UK/Melbourne, VIC: Cambridge University Press.

Marshall, T.H. (1963) 'Citizenship and social class', in T.H. Marshall *Sociology at the crossroads, and other essays*, London: Heinemann.

Mazzarol, T. and Soutar, G. (2002) 'Push-pull factors influencing student destination choice', *International Journal of Educational Management*, vol 16, no 2/3, pp 82-91.

Mills, M., Roseveare, J., Graham, B. and Mutch, L. (2005) *Impact of immigration policy on enrolments*, Wellington: Education New Zealand.

MOENZ (Ministry of Education, New Zealand) (2006) *Internationalisation in New Zealand tertiary education organisations*, Wellington: MOENZ.

MOENZ (2007) *International student enrolments in New Zealand, 2000-2006*, Wellington: MOENZ (www.educationcounts.govt.nz/publications/series/15260).

MOENZ (2010) *Code of Practice for the Pastoral Care of International Students* (Revised 2010), Wellington: Ministry of Education New Zealand.

MOENZ (2011a) *The code of practice*, Wellington: MOENZ (www.minedu.govt.nz/NZEducation/EducationPolicies/InternationalEducation/ForProvidersOfInternationalEducation/CodeofPracticeforInternationalStudents/CodeOfPractice.aspx).

MOENZ (2011b) *International student enrolments in New Zealand, 2004-2010* (www.educationcounts.govt.nz/publications/series/15260).

Moja, T., Muller, J. and Cloete, N. (1996) 'Towards new forms of regulation in higher education', *Higher Education*, vol 32, no 2, pp 129-55.

Mok, K.H. (2003) 'Globalisation and higher education restructuring in Hong Kong, Taiwan and mainland China', *Higher Education Research and Development*, vol 22, no 2, pp 117-29.

Mok, K.H. (2006) *Education reform and education policy in East Asia*, London/New York: Routledge.

Monash University (2008) *The education revolution:The lucky country can become the clever country*, Melbourne,VIC: Monash University http://www.go8.edu.au/__documents/media/go8-leaders/presentations/professor_larkins_press_club_270208.pdf).

Montgomery, C. and McDowell, L. (2009) 'Social networks and the international student experience: An international community of practice?', *Journal of Studies in International Education*, vol. 13, no. 4, pp. 455-66.

Moore, M.H. (1995) *Creating public value: Strategic management in government*. Cambridge, MA/London: Harvard University Press.

Murray, D. (2011) 'Envisioning the future global positioning of Australia in education, training and research', Paper prepared for national meeting with Australian Education International, Melbourne: International Education Association of Australia.

NAFSA: National Association of Internal Educators (2009) *Adviser's manual of federal regulations affecting foreign students and scholars*, Washington, DC: NAFSA (http://am.nafsa.org/regulatory_information.sec/nafsa_adviser_s_manual/aboutmanual).

Naidoo, V. (2009) 'Transnational higher education: A stocktake of current activity', *Journal of Studies in International Education*, vol 13, no 3, pp 310-30.

North, D.C. (1977) 'Markets and other allocation systems in history: The challenge of Karl Polanyi', *Journal of European Economic History*, vol 6, no 1, pp 703-16.

NUS (National Union of Students) (2010) 'Justice for international students', Carlton South,VIC: NUS (http://unistudent.com.au/site/index.php?option=com_content&view=article&id=47&Itemid=12).

Nussbaum, M.C. and Sen, A. (eds) (1993) *The quality of life*, Oxford: Clarendon Press.

Nyland, C., Forbes-Mewett, H. and Marginson, S. (2010) 'The international student safety debate: Moving beyond denial', *Higher Education Research and Development*, vol 29, no 1, pp 89-101.

Nyland, C., Forbes-Mewett, H., Marginson, S., Ramia, G., Sawir, E. and Smith, S. (2009) 'International student-workers in Australia: A new vulnerable workforce', *Journal of Education and Work*, vol 22, no 1, pp 1-14.

NZHRC (New Zealand Human Rights Commission) (2010) 'Comments of the New Zealand Human Rights Commission on New Zealand's implementation of the International Covenant on Economic, Social and Cultural Rights', Auckland: NZHRC (www2.ohchr.org/english/bodies/cescr/docs/.../NZHRC_PSWGCESCR46.doc).

NZHRC (2011a) 'Human Rights Commission', Auckland: NZHRC (www.hrc.co.nz/race-relations/te-ngira-the-nz-diversity-action-programme/participants-2012/human-rights-commission/).

NZHRC (2011b) 'Ensuring the safety of international students, Auckland: NZHRC (www.hrc.co.nz/news-and-issues/race-relations/ensuring-the-safety-of-international-students/).

NZQA (New Zealand Qualifications Authority) (2011) *Tertiary education*, Wellington: NZQA (www.nzqa.govt.nz/studying-in-new-zealand/tertiary-education/).

O'Brien, R., Goetz, A.M., Scholte, J.A. and Williams, M. (eds) (2000) *Contesting global governance: Multilateral economic institutions and global social movements*, Cambridge: Cambridge University Press.

OECD (Organisation for Economic Co-operation and Development) (1986a) *Flexibility in the labour market: The current debate*, Paris: OECD.

OECD (1986b) *Labour market flexibility: Report by a high-level group of experts to the Secretary-General*, Paris: OECD.

OECD (1988) *Employment outlook*, Paris: OECD.

OECD (1989) *Employment outlook*, Paris: OECD.

OECD (1990) *Labour market policies for the 1990s*, Paris: OECD.

OECD (2004a) *Internationalisation and trade in higher education: Opportunities and challenges*, Paris: OECD.

OECD (2008) *Education at a glance 2008*, Paris: OECD.

OECD (2010) *Education at a glance 2010*, Paris: OECD.

OECD (2011) *Education at a glance 2011*, Paris: OECD.

OIA (Office of the Independent Adjudicator) (2009) *Annual report 2008*, Reading: OIA (www.oiahe.org.uk/docs/OIAHE-Annual-Report-2008.pdf).

Olliffe, B. and Stuhmcke, A. (2007) 'A national university grievance handler? Transporting the UK Office of the Independent Adjudicator (OIA) to Australia', *Journal of Higher Education Policy and Management*, vol 29, no 2, pp 203-15.

Parker, C. and Braithwaite, J. (2003) 'Regulation', in P. Cane and M. Tushnet (eds) *The Oxford dictionary of legal studies*, Oxford: Oxford University Press, pp 119-45.

Parker, C., Scott, C., Lacey, N. and Braithwaite, J. (eds) (2004) *Regulating law*, Melbourne, VIC: Oxford University Press.

Partridge, M. (2010) 'Mixed reception', *Times Higher Education*, 23 December, pp 36-9.

Peters, M.A. (2007) *Knowledge economy, development and the future of higher education*, Rotterdam/Taipei: Sense Publishers.

Pierson, P. (1996) *Dismantling the welfare state? Reagan, Thatcher and the politics of retrenchment*, Cambridge, MA: Harvard University Press.

Pierson, P. (ed) (2001) *The new politics of the welfare state*, Oxford: Oxford University Press.

Polanyi, K. (1944) *The great transformation:The political and economic origins of our time*, Boston, MA: Beacon Press.

Poskanzer, S.G. (2002) *Higher education law:The faculty*, Baltimore, MD/ London: Johns Hopkins University Press.

Powell, M. (2007) *Understanding the mixed economy of welfare*, Bristol: Policy Press.

Ramia, G. (1998) 'Wage earners and "wage earners' welfare states": Industrial relations, social policy and social protection in Australia and New Zealand, 1890-1996', Unpublished PhD thesis, Sydney, NSW: School of Industrial Relations and Organisational Behaviour, University of New South Wales.

Ramia, G. and Carney, T. (2010) 'The Rudd Government's employment services agenda: Is it post-NPM and why is that important?', *Australian Journal of Public Administration*, vol 69, no 3, pp 263-73.

Ramia, G. and Wailes, N. (2006) 'Putting wage-earners into wage-earners welfare states: The relationship between social policy and industrial relations in Australia and New Zealand', *Australian Journal of Social Issues*, vol 41, no 1, pp 49-68.

Ramia, G., Marginson, S., Sawir, E. and Nyland, C. (2011) 'International business and cross-border education: A case of the Janus face of globalisation?', *Global Business and Economics Review*, vol 13, no 2, pp 105-25.

Ramsay, I.M. and Shorten, A.R. (1996) *Education and the law*, Sydney, NSW: Butterworths.

Rhodes, R. and Wanna, J. (2009) 'Bringing the politics back in: Public value in Westminster parliamentary government', *Public Administration*, vol 87, no 2, pp 161-83.

Rodan, P. (2009) 'The international student as student, migrant and victim', *Australian Universities Review*, vol 51, no 2, pp 27-31.

Rogowski, R. (1989) *Commerce and coalitions: How trade affects domestic political alignments*, Princeton, NJ: Princeton University Press.

Rosenau, J.N. (2000) 'Governance in a globalizing world', in D. Held and A. McGrew (eds) *The global transformations reader: An introduction to the globalisation debate*, Cambridge: Polity Press, pp 181-90.

Ross, J. (2009) '"Knee-jerk" regulations could scuttle international enrolments', *Campus Review*, vol 19, no 21, p 1.

Ross, J. (2011) 'India collapses, as international education moves to recycling phase', *Campus Review*, 23 May.

Sainsbury, M. (2011) 'Marketing blitz in Beijing', *The Australian*, 16 March.

Sassen, S. (2002a) 'Governance hotspots: challenges we must confront in the post-September 11 world', *Theory, Culture & Society*, vol 19, no 4, pp 233-44.

Sassen, S. (2002b) 'Towards post-national and denationalised citizenship', in E.F. Isin and B.S. Turner (eds) *Handbook of citizenship studies*, London: Sage Publications, pp 277-91.

Sassen, S. (2007a) *A sociology of globalisation*, New York/London: W.W. Norton & Co.

Sassen, S. (2007b) 'The places and spaces of the global: An expanded analytic terrain', in D. Held and A. McGrew (eds) *Globalisation theory: Approaches and controversies*, Cambridge: Polity Press, pp 79-105.

Sauvé, P. (2002) 'Trade, education and the GATS: What's in, what's out, and what's all the fuss about?', Paper prepared for the OECD (Organisation for Economic Co-operation and Development)/US Forum on Trade in Educational Services, 23-24 May, Washington, DC.

Sawir, E., Marginson, S., Nyland, C., Ramia, G. and Rawlings-Sanaei, F. (2009a) 'The pastoral care of international students in New Zealand: Is it more than a consumer protection regime?', *Asia Pacific Journal of Education*, vol 29, no 1, pp 45-59.

Sawir, E., Marginson, S., Nyland, C., Ramia, G. and Rawlings-Sanaei, F. (2009b) 'The social and economic security of international students: A New Zealand study', *Higher Education Policy*, vol 22, no 4, pp 461-82.

Scott, S. and Dixon, K.C. (eds) (2008) *The globalised university: Trends and challenges in teaching and learning*, Perth: Curtin University of Technology, Black Swan Press.

Sebastien, E. (2009) 'Protest from the fringe: Overseas students and their influence on Australia's export of education services policy 1983-96', Thesis submitted in partial fulfilment of the degree of PhD, University of Sydney.

Slaughter, A.M. (2004) *A new world order*, Princeton, NJ/Oxford, UK: Princeton University Press.

Smith, L. and Rae, A. (2006) 'Coping with demand: Managing international student numbers at New Zealand universities', *Journal of Studies in International Education*, vol 10, no 1, pp 27-45.

Spence, M. (2010) 'We need to use this crisis to do more for overseas students', *Sydney Morning Herald*, 12 February (www.smh.com. au/opinion/politics/we-need-to-use-this-crisis-to-do-more-for-overseas-students-20100211-nuzw.html).

Stanfield, J.R. (1980) 'The institutional economics of Karl Polanyi', *Journal of Economic Issues*, vol 14, no 3, pp 593-614.

Stilwell, F.J.B. (2006) *Political economy: The contest of economic ideas* (3rd edn), Melbourne, VIC: Oxford University Press.

Stuhmcke, A.G. (2001) 'Grievance handling in Australian universities: the case of the university ombudsman and the dean of students', *Journal of Higher Education Policy and Management*, vol 23, no 2, pp 181-9.

Swenson, P. (1991) 'Labor and the limits of the welfare state: The politics of intra-class alliances in Sweden and West Germany', *Comparative Politics*, vol 23, no 4, pp 379-90.

Swyngedouw, E. (2004) 'Globalisation or "glocalisation"? Networks, territories and rescaling', *Cambridge Review of International Affairs*, vol 17, no 1, pp 25-48.

Swyngedouw, E. (2005) 'Governance innovation and the citizen: The Janus face of governance-beyond-the-state', *Urban Studies*, vol 42, no 11, pp 1991-2006.

Tan, W. and Simpson, K. (2008) 'Overseas educational experience of Chinese students,' *Journal of Research in International Education*, vol 7, pp 93-112.

Teichler, U. (1999) 'Internationalisation as a challenge for higher education in Europe', *Tertiary Education and Management*, vol 5, no 1, pp 5-23.

Thelen, K. and Steinmo, S (1992) 'Historical institutionalism in comparative politics', in S. Steinmo, K. Thelen and F. Longstreth (eds) *Structuring politics: Historical institutionalism in comparative analysis*, Cambridge: Cambridge University Press, pp 1-33.

Think Before (2011) 'Are you feeling lucky?' (www.thinkbefore.com/).

Tomlinson, J. (1999) *Globalisation and culture*, Cambridge: Polity Press.

Trounson, A. (2011) 'International education sector braces for a fall', *The Australian*, 12 January.

UKCISA (UK Council for International Student Affairs) (2011) 'International students in the UK: Facts, figures – and fiction', London: UKCISA (www.ukcisa.org.uk/files/pdf/about/international_education_facts_figures.pdf).

UNESCO (United Nations Educational, Scientific and Cultural Organisation) (2011) 'Higher education mobility, quality and innovation' (http://portal.unesco.org/education/en/ev.php-URL_ID=12516&URL_DO=DO_TOPIC&URL_SECTION=201.html).

Universities Australia (2008) *Universities and their students: Principles for the provision of education by Australian Universities 2002*, Canberra, ACT: Universities Australia (www.universitiesaustralia.edu.au/documents/publications/Principles_final_Dec02.pdf).

Urias, D. and Yeakey, C.C. (2009) 'Analysis of the US student visa system', *Journal of Studies in International Education*, vol 13, no 1, pp 72-109.

ustream (2011) 'Unity in diversity',Video (www.ustream.tv/channel/unity-in-diversity-10-10-10).

Uvalic-Trumbic, S. (2002) 'Globalisation and quality in higher education: An introduction', in IAU (International Association of Universities), *Globalisation and the market in higher education*, Paris: UNESCO (United Nations Educational, Scientific and Cultural Organisation)/IAU, pp 1-8.

van Damme, D. (2002) 'Trends and models in international quality assurance in higher education in relation to trade in education', *Higher Education Management and Policy*, vol 14, no 3, pp 93-136.

Varghese, N.V. (2007) *GATS and higher education:The need for regulatory policies*, Research Papers, Paris: IIEP (International Institute for Educational Planning)/UNESCO (United Nations Educational, Scientific and Cultural Organisation).

VIWRC (Victorian Immigrant and Women's Refuge Coalition) (2011) 'Project update,Lost in Transition,Mate! Female international students tell stories in a video documentary',VIRWC (http://virwc.org.au/lost_in_transition/).

VUW (Victoria University of Wellington) (2011) *Legislation particularly applicable to Victoria University of Wellington*,Wellington:VUW (www.victoria.ac.nz/.../legislation-applicable-to-victoria-university.pdf).

Wailes, N. (2003) 'The importance of small differences: Globalisation and industrial relations in Australia and New Zealand', Unpublished PhD thesis, Sydney, NSW: Work and Organisational Studies, University of Sydney.

Wailes, N., Ramia, G. and Lansbury, R. (2003) 'Interests, institutions and industrial relations', *British Journal of Industrial Relations*, vol 41, no 4, pp 617-37.

Ward, C. and Masgoret, A.-M. (2004) *The experiences of international students in New Zealand: Report on the results of the national survey*, Wellington: Ministry of Education, New Zealand.

Watt, L. (2011) 'Dollar drive on the cards still', *The New Zealand Herald*, 25 September (www.nzherald.co.nz/tracking-the-nz-dollar/news/article.cfm?c_id=1501185&objectid=10754119).

Weber, M. (1921) *Economy and society*, Los Angeles, CA: University of California Press.

Weber, M. (1947) *The theory of social and economic organisation*, New York: Free Press.

Weiss, L. (1998) *The myth of the powerless state*, New York: Cornell University Press.

Wesley, M. (2009) 'Australia's poisoned alumni: International education and the costs to Australia', *Policy Brief,* Sydney, NSW: Lowy Institute for International Policy.

Woodward, S. (2010) 'Visit to help recover our international image', *Campus Review,* vol 20, no 19, p 9.

Xi, M. and Ning, G. (2006) *Christmas in summer: Chinese students in New Zealand*, Shenzhen, Guangdong: Haitian Publishing House.

Yeates, N. (2001) *Globalisation and social policy*, London: Sage Publications.

Yeates, N. (ed) (2008) *Understanding global social policy*, Bristol: Policy Press.

Zaphiriou, G.A. (1994) 'Introduction to civil law systems', in R.A. Danner and M.H. Bernal (eds) *Introduction to foreign legal systems*, New York/London/Rome: Oceania Publications, pp 47-55.

Ziguras, C. (2003) 'The impact of the GATS on transnational tertiary education: Comparing experiences of New Zealand, Australia, Singapore and Malaysia', *The Australian Educational Researcher,* vol 30, no 3, pp 89-109.

Ziguras, S. (2005) 'International trade in education services: Governing the liberalisation and regulation of private enterprise', in M.W. Apple, J. Kenway and M. Singh (eds) *Globalizing education: Policies, pedagogies, and politics*, New York: Peter Lang, pp 93-112.

Ziguras, C. and Law, S. (2006) 'Recruiting international students as skilled migrants: The global "skills race" as viewed from Australia and Malaysia', *Globalisation, Societies and Education*, vol 4, no 1, pp 59-76.

Index

Note: page numbers in *italic* type refer to tables.